Legacy: The Power Within

The Power of Thought Can:

Change Your Attitude

Change Your Behavior

Change your life

Legacy:
The Power Within

Tony DeLiso

Expanded Edition
www.powerlegacy.com

Writers Club Press
New York Lincoln Shanghai

Legacy: The Power Within

Writers Club Press
an imprint of iUniverse, Inc.

For information address:
iUniverse, Inc.
2021 Pine Lake Road, Suite 100
Lincoln, NE 68512
www.iuniverse.com

ISBN: 0-595-13520-X

Printed in the United States of America

Readers' Comments

"Legacy: The Power Within is thought provoking,—it clarifies and brings into focus the relationship between our thoughts and what we make happen in our lives."

Steve Bradbery
Software Engineer/Musician
Plantation, Florida

....

"I am sure Legacy: The Power Within will help create positive results in anyone's life who takes the time to absorb the powerful words within. I am sure it has affected mine."

Marilyn Dixon Pfanstiel, **Women Emerging Courageous**
Emerging Courageous Online Magazine
Lexington, Kentucky

....

"Creating positive outcomes in your life should be a legacy we all enjoy. Read Tony's book and inherit yours."

Nancy Brady
Program Assistant, Florida Atlantic University
Margate, Florida

....

"This book is to be read by those who truly want to be inspired and see the joy life has to offer. It's a reference manual for being a positive individual."

Dr. Samantha Lindmeier
Psychologist/Mother
Lady Lake, Florida

....

"Legacy: The Power Within inspires, guides, motivates and compels the reader to reach their goals with guidance from this knowledgeable and caring author."

Sandy Wagner
Adult ESL Instructor
Broward County Schools, Florida

....

"Legacy: The Power Within: Anyone who reads this book can gain insight into how to take control of their lives. It was on my "best gifts list" for all my family and friends."

Susan E. Vela
Regional Administrator
Downers Grove, Illinois

....

"Legacy: The Power Within keeps reminding us that, if we have the will to live, live it doing the right things not always for ourselves, but for others as well. That's where true love comes in like the famous saying 'To love your neighbor as you love yourself.'"

Jacqueline Thomas
Bookstore Manager
North Lauderdale, Florida

....

"Legacy: The Power Within, does exactly that, leaves you with power, understanding (that it IS your legacy), in such a way as to make the light go on inside your head! Simply stated, goal focused with logical and surefire ways to get there, successfully. Thanks, Tony."

Val Jennings
Key Concepts, Inc.
Contributing author to Success Is a Team Effort

....

"Legacy: The Power Within, captures the essence of faith, destiny, and courage, as it enlightens readers in search to find answers that appear closer to one's heart than one's set of eyes."

Jennifer Siller-Lasry
Author of Heartfelt Expressions
Fear and Faith: Heartfelt Expressions
Love Intertwines and Blessing of Closure

About..................

Legacy: The Power Within

It has been almost exactly four years since I had first started writing Legacy: The Power Within. In fact it was December of 1998 when I first began to write, and in December of 2002, I found myself motivated to start a new book. As I proceeded to write the new book, I found that what I was doing was writing more about the same subject as in the original edition of Legacy:...Something did not feel right. I was about seven pages into this "New Book" when I realized that what I was doing was something I had "intended" to do at some point after I finished my first book Legacy:..., and that was to write an expanded version of the same book. At that time I felt motivated to write, but I could not quite put my finger on what was bothering me with this new project. I did not really recognize the reason for the struggle I was having expressing myself in this new book. Most of the time my sub-vocalization went something like this.

"This is becoming a lot like the original Legacy: The Power Within, but I want to give it a little different slant. I want to write more about the ease with which peace and success can be achieved. But I don't want to write the same STUFF over." Well that was the kind of thinking (sub-vocalization) that was going on with me as I was writing.

As I mentioned, I was about seven pages into the "New Book" and I was becoming a little bit more frustrated at how laborious this writing was becoming. I also thought, how much it was like my previous work.

As I reflected a little on the time when I was writing Legacy: The Power Within, I remembered what I had previously intended for the original work. What I started to remember were my thoughts, and what my sub-vocalization was at that time. And that was, as I said, "I had intended to write an expanded version of the original book sometime in the future." So my subconscious, like yours, always listening and bring about what we think about, is why I am rewriting and expanding on the original book. It is what I asked for all of those years ago. And once again, I feel no struggle expressing myself in this "Old Book."

Although, I had always felt that I had written enough to help someone onto their path to finding "their way" to accomplish what they wanted to get out of life, I had wanted to say a little more. I expect that in this edition you will find that none of the basic material information has really been changed.

Let this "New Book" be another example of how the subconscious brings about what you think about into your life's reality.

About the Author

In 1948 I was born Antoniovito DeLiso, in a very old and small town in Italy called, Mola Di Bari. My father brought the family to the United States when I was barely one year old. I have been back to Italy to visit my warm and loving relatives only a few times since we moved.

My parents raised my older sister and me in Chicago. We lived in modest conditions in a very average neighborhood.

I attended public school throughout elementary, high school, and much later in life when I completed my college education. For the most part, my elementary school teachers had low expectation for what my future might hold. What I heard most of the time at parent/teacher conferences, and there were many, was, "He's smart, but he's lazy." "He doesn't pay attention; he's always starring out the window."

I barely managed to graduate high school and then I joined the Air Force. I did fairly well in the Air Force. I started to develop a sense of pride; that I could be someone, and that I could manage responsibility.

Since then, as my life moved forward with many trying times and a few encouraging words from others, I always sought to do better, to live a better life. I studied martial arts and yoga. I went to college and studied psychology and many years later I received a degree in business. Later still, I received a degree in teaching.

During all of those years what I truly wanted to know, what I was searching for, was the answer to the questions; who am I really? What is my relationship to "all that is," and what is spirit? I found my path by trial and error, like most of us do. Without my realizing it, all that I had done, all that I had studied, and all of the people who touched my life, just naturally brought me closer and closer to the answers to my questions. But a serious study of these questions brought me to writing this book. All of the great masters, sages, enlightened ones, and ordinary successful people seem to be saying the same thing. It is our legacy to bring into our lives, as Florence Scovel-Shinn might have put it; health, wealth, love, and perfect self-expression, just for the asking. I believe this legacy is within us all. Therein lays our personal power.

I wish to dedicate this book to my son, Vito, with love. At times I felt like I was coaching him in life as I wrote. At times it was as though some of our experiences together reminded me to include another section to discuss in this book.

I also wish to extend thanks to my son Vito and to Sara and Janet for their reflections on the original manuscript.

First of all I thank my parents Vito Antonio DeLiso and Carmela DeLiso for bringing me into this world. I thank them for doing the best they knew how in raising me. I thank them also for standing with conviction about their beliefs; else they could not have continued their love for one another and raised their family as they had. I thank them for creating the stability that they created in their lives with more than 53 years of marriage, which added to my sense of security, especially in my formative years.

I thank all of the people who have entered my life. For each of them have contributed to making me who I am today.

And to my childhood companion, my "Flying Seestor" Sara, whom, among other things, was often required to carry notes home to my mother from most of my elementary school teachers.

Contents

"I can Take It" Poem by, Vito DeLiso
"Forces of Good and Evil" Illustration by, Jennifer Canosa

My Best Wishes to All

*May Love, Health, Wealth, and Perfect Self-expression
be yours!*

Tony DeLiso

Introduction

To my view, my life still just keeps getting better and better. By that I do mean that peace, prosperity, and comfortable lifestyle, are ever increasing in my life. This too is what I sincerely wish that you, the reader, are saying as well.

As I stated, in this edition I have tried to change very little and added as much as I originally had intended to write. And as before, in this book I have included what I continue to teach, which is what I continue to practice, which is the driving force behind the writing of this material. This book is my personal confirmation of the power we, you and I, inherently posses. It is the great gift that we all have in common. This gift is the power from the one source in which we all share, and that gift is our **power of thought**.

When taken at its given literal value, this quote is one of the most powerful statements ever past down to us through ancient times: "Ask and you shall receive." I think it says it all. This quote was, and still is, the original basis for this book. Imagine, just ask and it can be yours. No strings attached. What can be more empowering?

As we examine the workings of this statement more closely we will find that from thought we create our lives. In thought, **desire, purpose, intention, belief, faith, and action,** are all the tools we need for the attainment of all that we want, all that we need to develop wondrous and fulfilling lives.

Let us look at this a little more closely. If your life is not going well, this is a signal, a good indication that your beliefs, your philosophy, may not be all that is best for you. It was fine in that it got you this far in life. But your personal evolution may have become stagnant. On the other hand, maybe you have just been miserable for such a long time, and now you are sick and tired of being sick and tired. Perhaps it is just time for you to make a few changes in your life, little or big, perhaps it is just time to make the changes.

If your are doing well in one area of your life and not so well in others, or if you are doing great and you wish to gain even more out of life, it is my belief that the material in this book and others like it, will in time and with practice, help you to bring about all that you desire in life. Having a wonderful life is your birthright.

In this, the expanded edition of Legacy: The Power Within, I have tried not to eliminate any of the original text and to keep this book as concise as possible, while knowing that more had to be said. There are some examples and quotes that I felt I could not leave out of this book. Examples, and even long drawn out explanations, are sometimes just necessary for teaching and setting a strong, lasting foundation on which to build.

For example: "Ask, believing, and you shall receive." Having said that this is one of the most empowering of statements handed down to us from the past, if you can understand and except this statement to be true, if you are using it to attain all of your desires and goals, then you do not need to read any further. You would of course continue to read and study if you are like me. It certainly helps if you just want to keep your mind centered and refreshed on the subject of who you really are, and the power that lies within you. This is probably the predominant reason that I keep studying. Yes, I continue to seek out lecturers and I continue to read the works of other authors as well. I have added to the original list of authors, a few more books that I have enjoyed reading.

There are great amounts of people in this country and all over the world that are suffering, miserable, or living discontented lives. I have chosen to avoid that path. I have chosen to help where I can. I feel that I cannot emphasize this next point enough. *I am writing to confirm that the legacy of these following concepts is at work for me. This information left to us from past generations has helped millions of people all over the world to prosper, and it will continue to help others as well.*

I have divided the material in this book into sections of discussion. The first section, and I feel the most important, is about understanding and building a strong philosophical, and psychological foundation that works. Philosophy is the study of life; search for truth. This is true in any subject of study. Psychology is the study of the workings of the mind. It is the study of the psyche, originally the study of soul or spirit.

Next, is a brief section using a formal step-by-step method of goal setting. This section is intended to help you to formulate a clear idea of what you desire to achieve.

The third section is about developing a circle of influence. This is a discussion on the value and the importance of creating a network of friends and business associates.

Following that is a discussion on affirmations. Affirmations are clearly thought out statements. They are the internal dialog on purpose with purpose, which are the basis for all success. Daily affirmations help you to hold, maintain, and guide you, toward your visions and the attainment of your goals. As with prayer, affirmations are a working method of communication with the Self. They have been used for thousands of years to purposefully communicate with the subconscious mind to reach: Infinite Intelligence, Universe, Higher Self and yes God.

I have included in this book a short autobiography, should you be interested in knowing a little bit about me, a summary of facts that are brought out in this book, and a meditation exercise that I use.

In my section of acknowledgment and appreciation to those wonderful writers and teachers who have carried on the message of the legacy, I have included their names and their book titles of which I have studied and enjoyed. Again, of course I have added a few more titles in this expanded edition. The study of these books has brought within me peace and a working knowledge of the process for achieving success. Moreover, these writings have given me a new perspective on concepts that I have heard of all my life, but that had little or no meaning for me until now. My hope is that along with this book, they may do the same for you as they have for me and more.

SECTION ONE

Clearing the Ground

Clearing the Ground to Lay the Foundation

My intention is to continue "The Legacy"

This is a book about understanding concepts that have brought about health, wealth, love, and perfect self-expression, to millions of people around the world. These concepts did not originate from me. My intention is to carry on this information. I want to share what I have learned with as many people as I can reach through this book and the seminars I conduct.

The knowledge that I am passing on, though ancient and timeless, has worked for me in helping me to attain my goals and to create for myself a more peaceful and more prosperous life. This knowledge that I wish to share with you has brought me a more orderly and successful lifestyle, a life in which wonders truly never cease. I would like you to know this can be true for you as well.

Here is another bit of wisdom. "You shall know the truth and the truth shall set you free" (John 8:23). You are given the tool of thought from birth. When you learn to use the power of thought to enjoy your life, and you start to realize who you really are, you will cease to be bound (as in, tied up) to the burdens of life. I think you will begin to see much more of life's wonders.

Why would these concepts work for everyone as they have been working for me? These concepts must work for everyone, because we are all made from the same "Star Stuff." Therefore, it is my belief and from my experience, that you too can know fulfillment of life through the understanding and practice of these concepts.

To paraphrase the works of Florence Scovel-Shinn, it is your Divine Right to have a life of wealth, health, love, and perfect self-expression; in perfect ways, under Grace.

I have found that by changing my mind, that is to say, changing my old and untrue beliefs to beliefs that work, I have changed my life. In doing so, ridding my mind of old and untrue beliefs has given me more control over my life, and more peace of mind. And of course, I will explain how you too can change your mind and take control of your life.

The legacy that is passed on here is the knowledge that this is your life to do with what you choose to do with it. You are here to co-create and express your being. No matter what status you have achieved in this life, there is always room for growth, new goals, and challenges. One of the most important aspects of this legacy is that you do not have to live a life of strife and hardships.

This is a book about understanding the relationship between you and your-Self; to encourage you to keep on seeking to discover who you really are. I hope you will find that you can be glad, grateful, and amazed at what your life can be.

Laying the Foundation

Mind and Body

Let us start with this concept. There is a conscious you and a subconscious you.

For example, think of an ice-burg. When you look at an ice-burg, you see so little of what is actually there. The conscious you is like the obvious part of the ice-burg which we call "the tip." While, the subconscious you would be that overwhelmingly larger part hidden from sight.

Who you are and what you are on Earth are basically a mind and a body. Both of these aspects of you are so perfectly, complexly, and intricately designed. Yet to start with, to maintain good physical health, the body only needs a little routine exercise, good food, and regular periods of rest, of which I will discuss further on in this book.

To continue, the "you" that we call the conscious mind, seeks to create, to live in harmony, and to find peace and happiness. All you need to function and grow in good health is a Little Conscious Effort on your part. That seems to be a simple enough statement to take much of the stress out of life. Why have I made certain to mention a Little Conscious Effort? Let me answer the question this way.

So again, your mind is basically divided into two parts, with many complex aspects and physiology, the obvious part and the not so obvious part. But just the same, your mind is made up of two main aspects and they are of course both you. Stated in its simplest terms again, they are the conscious you and the subconscious you. (See, Dr. Joseph Murphy, *The Power of the Subconscious Mind*) Simplest terms yes, but volumes have been written on this subject and stated in many ways for eons, yes thousands of years.

To help simplify for our purpose, and in reality, let us say the conscious you is the "you" that is reading, watching a movie, maintaining your household, working, studying, and sensing your environment through your five senses. Consciously you also think and make decisions constantly about what you will do or what you will not do, what you like or what you do not like.

On the other hand, so to speak, the subconscious part of your mind has the larger role in your life-works. First of all, it never needs rest and so it never sleeps. It keeps every function of your body running in perfect order down to replacing and rebuilding every cell that makes up your entire body, even as you go on about your daily routine. As an example, the conscious you does not worry about at how many beats per minute your heart is working, that is the job of your subconscious mind. This is true about all of what we call our involuntary muscles that compose our digestive system, liver, pancreas, lungs, and all of the neurological chemical-electrical system of your body. They are all, and at all times, being carefully monitored and coordinated by your subconscious mind. This is a part of you that until now you literally may not have been aware even existed.

Your subconscious mind has so many other subtle aspects about it. That is to say, the discoveries and theories that so many scientists, theologians, and your everyday success oriented people have brought into light through study, research, and the many books made available to us.

It is said by some that your subconscious mind is located in the region of your solar plexus, or also known as the area of your heart and just below it. Understandably so, because this is the area of your physical body in which you feel affected by emotional stresses. For example, the affects you have from the feelings of love, hate, and anger are felt in this region with most people. I am certain that you have heard the phrases, "Think with your heart" or "This comes form my heart."

The feeling you get when this happens is what is called a "visceral feeling." The feeling that you have may be wonderful, sad, discomforting or even fearful. To describe this feeling we might use phrases like: "I have a bad feeling in the pit of my stomach about this." "I had a good hunch this would work out, so I just went for it!" "I just knew" this or that would happen, "I had a gut feeling."

These varying feelings are being communicated to you by your subconscious mind and for a purpose. One purpose may be just to help you to become aware of the fact of the communication process itself. If you are not now aware of this fact, then with time and practice you may come to recognize that there is communication going on between your conscious you and your subconscious you.

Fact: "Your subconscious mind is always alert and communicating with you." It finds ways to communicate with you. Sometimes the subconscious uses subtle ways to communicate, and sometimes through those hard and difficult situations we go through in life that seems to take forever to overcome. We call these situations "Life's Lessons," like when it is time for us to move on with our lives, but we may have been reluctant or unwilling to make the necessary changes. Then, things seem to happen that may be very difficult to manage, and sometimes even tragic. We humans do have a tendency to avoid change until we find that we are forced to change; "to move on."

As I alluded to earlier, there are many people who, until now, in their search for understanding something about their lives, have not realized this other aspect of themselves, this other mind concept. Yet, once this other mind concept is accepted, then it is to be understood, it is all still "you" that we are discussing. I think after that, the hardest part is to recognize the fact that there really is no separation. So for clarity, let us look at these three aspects. 1. The mind is made up of two parts, the conscious and the subconscious. 2. There is constant communication at work between the conscious and the subconscious. 3. And, it is all still "You."

The communication factor works well when we think of the subconscious as another being. For practice, and at least for the immediate future, you might try this: I would like you to consider thinking of your subconscious as your very best friend, brother, sister, mother, father, confidant or et cetera. Again for practice, use your imagination and actually talk to this "Best Friend" of yours.

Your subconscious, the higher-you, answers questions, leads and directs you in countless ways through your feelings, your dreams, the urges you get, the books you read, movies, and through the people you know now and those you will be lead to meet in the future. All of this is for your benefit. All of this is for your growth, and all for your highest good.

Another factor to be very aware of is that since the communication is constantly on going, **you do communicate with your subconscious mind constantly, and with your habit thinking as well.** Your subconscious wants you to know, it is not a one way conversation that you are having. It is **listening to you all of the time,** and responding all of the time (I cannot say this often enough).

As you become more aware of this relationship you will begin to realize that it has **always** given you what you have "asked for." As I was learning about this communication, this **"always"** factor disturbed me. I never asked for a divorce. I never asked to lose my job, my business, nor had I asked to lose my house. I never asked to be sick. I never asked for all of those hard times, lack of money, or lack of love. I also did not realize how closed off I was to people; how dense or stubborn I was to accepting reality. In other words, I really did not realize how negative my thinking was; that I caused my life to be the way it was.

The best reasons I can think of for making a constant practice of understanding the relationship that exist within and between your conscious and subconscious mind, is to discover who you really are and this innate power which is yours. It starts with the development of harmonious thinking between your conscious and subconscious mind, thereby affording you to lead a wondrous and amazing life. **Therefore, we seek and develop the power from within ourselves.**

Belief-Attitude-Behavior

Belief

"What you think about you bring about."

Affect your subconscious and your life will change to what ever you want it to be.

Now that we have something of an understanding of the relationship between the conscious and subconscious Self, let us delve a little further. Whether or not you believe in God, Infinite Intelligence or a Higher Power, this in itself may not keep you from having successes in your life. And, not to be contradictory, but as a matter of concept, I believe you will find more peace when you look inside and beyond yourself for success. Belief in yourself is an excellent place to start, if you believe in nothing else.

Success means so many different and not so different things to so many people. I find for myself that success means, a peaceful resolve in bringing about a desire to fruition with satisfaction of accomplishment.

First understand this as best as you can. Fact: The one thing you have **total control over is your mind.** That is to say, you have control over your thinking and the ability to change your thinking. This cannot be stated too often either. If you have free will, it is in the choices you make in your thinking. You can choose to think positively or you can choose to hold on to your negative and judgmental beliefs.

Your belief system constitutes your attitude and your behavior, in that order, and this constitutes the conditions and circumstances of your life.

What you believe about yourself and your world around you, creates the world around you. Like it or not, you are the power behind what your life's conditions and circumstances are like. "What you think about you bring about." This quote is true and always has been true. It is your God-given birthright to have this kind of power and dominion over your life.

Let me briefly explain how this works and what you can do to consciously use your birthright to your advantage.

How do we develop our beliefs? We learn with and from our environment. We learn through our five senses in the form of symbols from the time we are born. These symbols are then imprinted in our brain as sort of a storage file of information. As we grow, and through our innate desire to communicate, we learn the language of our environment (culture) and translate the symbols into words; thus eventually we learn what is good or bad and to become judgmental. Up until that point we are basically observers of our environment and things just happen (not by accident), and we feel. We feel and we know that we are. This is an aspect of the conscious mind.

Here is the tricky part. After we have become pretty good at thinking, using words, and we have become pretty good at using language, we begin to become pretty good at believing those around us that we trust, primarily our caretakers. This has a tremendous affect on what we believe and then the reverse happens. We then turn words into symbols (beliefs) that are impressed into our brains (subconscious), and thus we take an active part in developing our beliefs. From this, we develop our conditions and circumstances. Putting it into the simplest form that I can, we go from observers to the creators of our daily lives, because of the way we think about the things we think about and the way in which we judge these thoughts. That is the short version of where and how our conscious power begins.

Nobody usually tells us this, because we would have to take responsibility for the way we think, the way that we live, and that our lifestyle, if it is not wonderful, is something that we have created. (People with wonderful lives don't seem to mind taking credit for their lives being so wonderful). We are taught that there are plenty of people and circumstances to blame if our lives are not wonderful. We are taught much of this kind of thinking by others who were taught the same thing, and this becomes a cycle passed on through generations. This is a cycle that you can break, if you really have the desire to break it. Well, if we have created our lives the way they are, and we do not like the way we are living, then we can recreate it. Yes you can, but you really have to have the desire to change!

If your beliefs and behavior (action) are not bringing you the kinds of results (events and experiences) you wish to have in your life__ look first to your beliefs and behavior.

You cannot do a thing (an action) unless it is in alignment with your beliefs. If you do, you will probably feel guilt, shame or any number of other negative feelings. The fact that you cannot take an action that is contrary to your beliefs has been found to be true when someone undergoes hypnosis.

If you are really responsible for circumstances and events in your life, the cause of the events and structure of your life, then you should have the power and ability to change these events to your liking. And again, **you do have this power and ability.** In order to affect the changes in your life that you desire to have, you first have to change your beliefs, at least to some extent anyway. Can you affect change in your beliefs, or is it really too late? Since these negative or useless beliefs have been with you all of your life, you may already believe this change to be impossible to do, but it is not! Yes, you can affect change in your beliefs. And, you have been doing so all along about one thing or another anyway. Based on the Universal Law of Change, even the most stubborn, resistant to change personality, does change to some degree.

The first step you have to take in changing your life for the better, to something more prosperous and full of wonder, is to **change your beliefs.** This is accomplished by becoming **aware of your thinking;** become **aware** of what your beliefs are. To do that, you may start by looking at the conditions and circumstances in and of your life for clues. Ask yourself some questions; questions that in fact, no one else but you can answer. Are you comfortable with your lifestyle? Do you have enough love, friendship, money, good health, and an outlet for perfect self-expression? Are you doing the things you want to do in life? If not, then you will need to look at making changes on purpose, with purpose, to help you to change the way you look at things and to affect change in your thinking. It is a simple process, but not always very easy to accomplish. This is how you will learn to become the cause of the life you wish to lead, instead of being the "cause" because of your reactions to events and opportunities that occur. By the way, events and opportunities will occur in your life daily based on your habit thinking. When your need to make changes becomes great enough, you will become aware of the necessity to change, but why wait?

When you become aware of the power that you really have, it is important to accept it and try to understand it. We all have this tremendous power. It is not something to feel guilty about, because it is your God-given right to have it and to use it for your highest good, or, in any other manner in which you choose.

Off hand there are two aspects that cause the feeling of guilt due to this power. The feeling of guilt that comes from thinking that it is egotistical to think that "I have the power of a god," or that "I am like God." The other aspect is the guilt for some that comes from not having taken responsibility sooner, for this "wonderful gift of power that I have," as though they may have offended God in some way for not knowingly using this power. Shed the guilt. In either case you have not offended God.

If you are looking around you at the success of others, your friends' successes, you are becoming aware. When you become sick and tired of being sick and tired of the way your life is going, you will become aware. You do not have to wait until you get to this point in your life, but the fact is that many of us do. Do you have to discover what all of your beliefs are before you can move forward toward a better and more satisfying life? No, absolutely not. While you are looking, contemplating and understanding, you can move on to the next step, and that is, "practice asking."

The second step is to create a **strong desire** to have the successes you want to attain and deserve in life. A strong desire in itself will start you on your way toward making the changes in your beliefs and thinking, which will, in turn, put you on your way to your right path and to your successes in your endeavors. Desire, in itself, will put in motion your creative imagination faculties that will tremendously enhance the attainment of the end results you have chosen. I will talk more on the effects and importance of desire later on as we continue.

The third, and a very powerful step in changing your beliefs so they will benefit you, is to change your behavior through your actions. Yes, to a great extent your beliefs will begin to change by repetition of positive behavior. **Caution: Pretending won't get it, but acting will.** I will discuss this point further, but first, let us look at attitude.

Create for yourself a calm attitude about living your life.

"Your ship comes in over calm waters." (Shinn)

Order in the Universe is not an accident. If you look closely at it, even chaos can be argued to seem orderly. Everything in the universe is intended to flow with ease. I will discuss this further, as well.

For now let me say this, if your life is not flowing in a manner which is carefree, perhaps you have not given enough care and attention to the things for which you have taken responsibility. Become aware of your life. Look at your relationships. Is there harmony? Are your bills paid? Do you have enough to eat? Are you taking care of…? The fact is that, if you are taking good care of these aspects, then your life is smooth sailing and carefree. Are you doing all that you need to do so that there are no worries in your life?

Attitude

Radiate Love and Love is What You Will Attract.
Radiate Success and Success is What You Will Attract.

I must interject here, that if you radiate Fear, Doubt, Anger, and et cetera, you will, by the Law of Attraction, cause yourself to experience more fear, doubt, anger, and et cetera.

Attitude is what you project of yourself outwardly to be your disposition and personality. It is based on your belief system, that is, it is based on what you believe to be true about yourself and the world around you. Attitude is what and how you radiate, that other people perceive you to be.

Attitude falls under the Universal Law of Attraction. For example: I am sure that at some point in your life, you have found that you really liked or did not like someone, but that you had no strong reasons for your feelings of which you were aware. Perhaps you had just met that person. One of the most predominant of reasons for these feelings, let us say the feeling of dislike, is because of what they are radiating about who and what they are at that time, which may be an aura of negativity, or a fear that they are projecting. What you radiate is what you attract and you repel its opposite. An example of attraction would be of course those people with whom it seems everyone enjoys being around. Then there are those who being envious or negative in some way, thus cause repulsion.

In some instances, we confuse attitude with behavior, because how we radiate is so closely aligned with how we act, attitude is almost considered to be a behavioral pattern. Fact: Your belief about yourself and your world around you is radiated through your attitude. It is a strong reflection of your belief, and an indication of how and why you act the way you do.

If you wish to attract wonderful people and opportunities, then dig inside yourself to affect change in how and what you radiate. You can radiate that wonderful person of which you already are, and open your-self up to the wonderful experiences that must follow in time.

Like attracts like and repels all else. As is said, "Birds of a feather flock together."

Behavior/Action

Of these three facets; belief, attitude, and behavior; behavior is seem-ingly the most obvious indicator of your beliefs, because it is the most tangible. Certain behaviors are even measurable, which is an important factor in goal setting, of which I will discuss later on in this book. If you look at how a person acts, their actions will give you clues as to their beliefs. Some examples might be, the way they adorn their bodies, where and how they live, where and how they work and play, and what a person will or will not do, are all indicators of their belief system.

Our behavior is and can only be a reflection of that which we believe is true about ourselves and of the world around us. Again, as is found to be true under hypnosis, a person cannot do or be made to do something that goes against their beliefs. In other words, they cannot be made to do some-thing that they consciously just would not do on their own.

One major benefit of acting out our lives is that it does not take a spe-cialist to recognize behavior that is positive or behavior that is negative. You either like the way someone acts or you do not. Someone who truly cares about you or your performance in a given situation, may tell you that, in there opinion, you are not acting on your own best behalf, or on theirs. Well, what can you do about it? You are only acting based on the way you believe, which is based on your environment and the manner in which you were raised. Although this is true, it is also true that you can change your beliefs by modifying your actions. Likewise, you either like the circumstances and conditions in and of your life, or you do not.

Let us discuss acting for a moment. The best and award winning actors in show business are those who literally take-on the role of a character that they are portraying. The list of actors is fairly large who do get into their roles well, but to *Be* someone else in a play or in a movie, that list of actors becomes shorter. As examples, Dustin Hoffman in "Rain Man" and Tom Hanks in "Forrest Gump" stand out in my mind. They do not pretend to be someone else; they portray the character in truth, as truth. It does not matter if your favorite actor is **taking-on** the part of the hero or the part of a villain. If their role becomes believable to you the audience, then you yourself become involved in the drama as though it were real. Most often this effect is known as, "The willing suspension of disbelief." This is another psychological phenomenon that allows us to enjoy watching a play or a movie and except it as though it were really happening. Of course, in real-life observing an act of slapstick or murder, to say the least, is not nearly as easy to witness as it is in a movie or in a play.

You too can become an actor and take-on the role of a *successful person*, for example. In effect, you can decide on a role-model, someone whose success and whose lifestyle is like that which you would like to emulate, desire to copy, to have for yourself. You can **act** in a similar fashion as they do. Make that type of lifestyle a reality for yourself, by affecting change in your beliefs and rewriting the script of your life to something more desirable to you.

Pick out the qualities of several well-to-do people and act as they would act. Study! Study people of success and do the things they have done. You may find that you can improve on what they have accomplished, or at the very least improve your own lifestyle. Some businesses and sales organizations call this method of acting, "Fake it 'til you make it." In essence, you portray yourself as successful and do the things that someone you admire in your chosen field of endeavor might do. And then, become aware of the successful changes in your life.

It is important to give yourself time to think about what you would really desire to accomplish. Decide on the end result of what you want to achieve. If you want something, do something that you think will bring about the results that you want, and then **expect** to get what you want.

Fact: Action always gets a reaction and doing always gets results. If you do not like the results you get from the action you have chosen, take another approach; do it differently. Use your imagination and choose to do something else.

One of the strongest methods used to modify your **belief system** is to affect your subconscious mind by action. Affect your subconscious and your life will change to whatever you want it to be.

Subconscious

I believe, as did Napoleon Hill, "The possibilities of creative effort connected with the subconscious mind are stupendous and imponderable. They inspire one with awe."

The subconscious is likewise known by some as The Soul, the cause of who we are and that we are. It is the "You" that makes things happen, the "You" whom you are. Some say the subconscious is your slave. It is said that it will bring you what ever you ask for into your life. It is not my intention to debate this matter; the end result is the same. It has come to be my belief that the subconscious part of us is our innate power. *It is our Divine Right to have this power and use it all of the time.*

Will you always get what you ask for from your subconscious? In a manner of speaking, yes you will. Valuable scriptures from the past attest to this fact. Since the subconscious mind has overwhelming resources and knowledge we do not consciously have, since it knows why we are here on Earth in the first place, since it knows our needs better than we do, sometimes the answer is no, not right now. Moreover, sometimes some of our experiences will seem extremely harsh to us as well, mostly due to incorrect beliefs and behavior. These are the more difficult experiences in life. They are generally caused by following the ego and engaging in thoughts of fear, lack, and worry.

Much has been written about the subconscious as a storehouse for memories that contribute to positive and negative attitudes. It is, as I have stated, the place from where our power stems. Some writers have even called it your slave or describe it to be like a genie in a lamp. It will bring you opportunities and things based on what you have asked for in thought, spoken word or by your actions, and of course based on your daily habits of thought and behavior.

For example: If you are a negative thinker by habit, judgmental about people and situations, through your subconscious you will attract more negative experiences to yourself. If you are happy with yourself, if you like people and the world around you in general, then through your subconscious you will attract more positive experiences.

The job of the subconscious is to "bring about that which you think about." Your thoughts, wishes, and judgments are "yours." And therefore, YOU are by Divine Right, responsible for your life. The subconscious does not try to second-guess you. Let us say it just arranges the conditions and circumstances or things to be in your life as you see your life to be.

My friend, you are not trapped or doomed to live in situations and circumstances which you do not like. Remember! You have **total control over your mind.** That is to say, what you think about, and what you fill your mind with, is your choice. This is similar to the old fashion teaching of computer programming, "garbage in—garbage out." What you allow to enter into your thoughts, what you are impressing your subconscious mind with, will eventually show up in your life.

Let us look again at this book as an example. I was contemplating the writing of the expanded edition of this book four years ago. As I said in the beginning, I started to write what I thought was going to be another book. The material I began to write was causing me to become frustrated. What I started to write about also reminded me of my original thought, which of course was to expand on the original edition. As I worked to expand my original book I realized that the project flowed more smoothly again, because this is where my motivation is; not on writing a new and very different book. Again, back then, when I was writing my original book, I knew I would someday write a somewhat longer version. This was what I had impressed my subconscious mind that I wanted to do.

Things happen in your life because they are supposed to happen, and of course based on the condition and circumstances you create by your thinking. It is so important that you be very discerning about the way you choose to live, who you choose to associate with, the materials that you read, movies you watch, and et cetera. You do not have to like or dislike anything or anybody; just decide on that which is for your highest good. Decide with whom and with what you will surround yourself. You will by virtue of these facts, start to attract more of the best things in life to yourself.

Changing your life to what you want it to be starts with being **aware** of your **self** and your surroundings. I do not think I can emphasize this point often enough. Stop periodically and take the time to ask yourself some simple questions. Are you satisfied with your living conditions and the circumstances in your life? These surroundings are the reflections of your mind and of your thinking. Are you disorganized? Do you let your car become messy for long periods of time? Do you procrastinate? The conditions and circumstances in your life are the direct results of your daily thinking habits. You have nothing to lose and everything you desire to gain, if you will open your mind to change for your highest good.

Continuous awareness is the key to recognizing that a change is needed. As I stated earlier, you can choose to make the changes. Continue asking yourself the important questions. Do you like the way your life is going? Do you live in wonderful surroundings? Do you have creditors at your heels for payments due to them? Do you like your job?

What about the people with whom you associate? They are a reflection of you too, and of your habit thinking. By the Universal Law of Attraction, you have drawn these people into your life. Do your friends and associates drain you of your energy with their constant complaints about other people, their family problems, their jobs, and their lives? Do these friends have worthwhile goals? Do you see these friends seeking new and wonderful experiences? Do you see purpose and growth in their lives?

Once you have decided to take control of your life by taking control of your thoughts, you can purposefully begin to impress your subconscious to bring you all the good that is rightfully yours! Life is like a giant department store filled with anything you can imagine that you could want to have for yourself. As you walk through this giant department store of life, you imagine and see all of the wondrous things available for you to have. "Oh if only I could have that job, or that boat, or that car, or that house." Your subconscious mind's job is to bring about into your life, the opportunities for you to have whatever is your heart's desire, just for the asking. (And yes, some of the things you ask for may take time to receive.)

This brings us back to, how are you asking? This is one of the most important aspects of the quote, "Ask and you shall receive." Do you ask with faith, which is expectation, that you will receive what you have asked? Or, are you concluding your request with some negating thought? This of course brings us back to **awareness** of how you are thinking. Remember! What you receive daily in your life is based on your habit thinking. It is a reflection of what you think about and how you think about what you think about, and of this, is what you want to become aware. Remember too, that your subconscious mind does not second-guess you. It sets out to bring you what you are asking for, even in your thinking.

Here is a thought. "I really desire abundance in my life, **but**, I know I'm not worthy of it yet." Is this not a typical message so many of us receive through our associations and our environments as we move through life from our very early childhood? And then, we send out this negating thought along with our desires for good to be manifested; what gets manifested into your reality is what you believe most. Like, "Yeah, I want abundance **but**…" Doesn't "but" negate all the nice things we said prior to "but?" How does this sound to you? "I love your new dress, but…"

It is true that we do build our beliefs based on who and to what we are exposed. Some of us are programmed with such notions as, "We are not worthy of love unless we prove ourselves worthy." What should you have to prove or to give to receive love, except to give love itself? Or, "We are not worthy of success until we have paid our dues." What should you need to pay for success except honest service in your work and relationships? So then, what do you need to do to bring forth abundance in your life? You came into this life with all the necessary tools to develop abundant living, good health, love, and perfect self-expression. All that is required for you to receive what is basically your right to live well is your desire, faith, and action. Then, pay attention to what is going on in your life and you will be guided or drawn to the life you want and deserve. (Unusual as it may seem to be perhaps, but sometimes the only actions required are the "thinking and receiving.")

To create for ourselves a more abundant and successful life, we can rebuild our beliefs with what we purposely expose ourselves.

The things that most strongly affect your subconscious mind are your **declared** desires, intentions, emotions, faith, and actions. **A clearly stated or declared** desire is probably the strongest of prayers that you will ever make. With this, your conscious mind and your subconscious mind understand exactly what you really are asking. Send out your request to the Universe, your Higher-Self, or God unencumbered with a lot of worry and other negating thoughts. Then your subconscious mind will immediately proceed to arrange for you to receive your request. Get out of your own way, so to speak, and let it happen. Repeat your request often knowing that you will receive what you have asked to be manifested into your life. With that, your subconscious will even guide you and develop in you the drive you will need to do your part.

Your intention, emotions, faith, and actions are an extremely important source of power in the attainment of your request. Furthermore, they all stem from your desire to receive and/or achieve what ever it is that you are asking to be brought into your life.

Remember always: Your habit thinking, positive or negative, even in jest, (with humor) causes in your life for you to attract to you, what you have and to be what it is. These next examples show ownership of what your thoughts are saying: "I do the dumbest things sometimes." "I'm not worthy..." "I'm such a jerk." "You're a pain in the neck." "You'd think I'd learn by now..." "Today is going to be a really bad day; I can just feel it already." "I think I'm going to be ill." Again, "What you think about you bring about." Even if consciously you do not think you mean it, you will impress your subconscious with these common phrases and all thoughts. Your subconscious mind does not second-guess you. Your subconscious will confirm and make these thoughts a reality for you.

You do not have to wait until you have totally cleansed your mind to start reshaping your life to what you want it to be. Just start doing it! Begin by filling your mind with thoughts for improving your life; thoughts that may bring to you your highest good.

In time, with practice and awareness of your thinking, you will have more positive thoughts than you have of those that are negative thoughts. This cleansing, for example, would be like taking a glass of stained water, perhaps stained with ink. If you were to keep pouring clean, clear water into that glass, it will eventually become much clearer. Likewise, as you practice awareness of your thinking, and expose yourself to more positive thoughts and experiences, this same kind of clearing of fearful and negating thoughts will happen for you in your mind. During the day as you become aware that you are having a negative thought, just gently send it on its way. Do not rebuke yourself for having this kind of thought, just release it. Simply cease giving it your attention. Your conscious and subconscious thinking, along with your habit thinking, will produce for you the wonderful life you so richly deserve.

A positive attitude is one that is free of fears and negative thoughts.

How a simple thing like changing my thinking has changed my life.

Simple yes, easy no, at least it has not been easy for me. I thought I was rid of fears and negative thinking. I really thought so! I thought of myself as a pretty stable guy. I could not think of what I might be afraid of that I could not resolve. So, "what's there to fear?"

"Seek first the Kingdom of Heaven…" This is the starting point.

Spend the time to get to know who you are; your relationship with your own spirit, with Infinite Intelligence, with the universe and your subconscious mind.

How do you develop a wonderful, amazing life of success in achieving your goals? Simple, by assessing your beliefs and developing a positive belief system, you can achieve and attain anything you can imagine. This may not be easy at first, but it is simple, and with practice you will get better at it. To do that, you might begin with **awareness**. Start by assessment of where you are now and what you would like to accomplish, or how you would like to redesign your life to be.

Reflection

Reflection is one of the most valuable mental tools you have at your disposal to accomplish this first step. Before you even begin goal setting, give yourself some time to think about **what** and **how** you are thinking. Through reflection you can become aware of your daily thinking and living habits. You may have to re-read this next statement over to gain its meaning. Reflect on what you think about and how you think about what you think. Do this often.

We are constantly involved in an internal dialog. Identify what it is you are thinking and saying to yourself. In other words, by reflection assess is your thinking positive, or negative in nature? This is **one of the most** important aspects of the your ability to succeed in goal setting, regardless of your definition of success, or of getting what you want out of life.

Reflection is the process by which you are going to become aware of a thing known by some as **sub-vocal expression.** This is the silent voice from within you (not from deep within you).

Sub-vocal expression can actually be detected by minuscule muscular movement in the larynx corresponding to the words you are forming in your mind. Even right now as you read, and often without your being aware you are doing it, there is this muscular movement found in your throat. You may notice that with some people they even move their lips to the train of words they are thinking. And yet with some others, their thoughts are almost audible as they whisper what they are thinking. While with still others, they may speak out as they are thinking, like in this common expression, "I was just thinking out loud."

So then, the first step is to reflect and become aware of your thoughts. Thoughts are constantly flowing in and out of your consciousness. If you pay attention to your thoughts, often you will find positive and negative thoughts in the form of fantasy scenarios. You create in your mind responses to events as they occur, or as they might occur in your mind and in your life. You may find too, that you are rehashing good or bad experiences in your mind, as in, when you are daydreaming of past experiences.

Try this. Sit quietly and just become aware of your thoughts. As you reflect, assess where you are now and what you would like to accomplish, or how you would like to redesign your life to be. Think, or you might write down your thoughts for this exercise. At any rate, your function during this process will be to pay close attention to how you respond to your thoughts on a given subject.

I am going to purposely use the term MY in this very simplistic example. You can start by asking yourself some of these questions. **"How do I feel about my** job, my boss, my significant other, my car, my life, etc?" When you have asked yourself this series of questions, you will naturally respond in your own mind as to what you think and feel about each situation. What did you answer? You did answer! Was there a positive or a negative response in your thinking? Did you feel a sting or a discomfort after having a thought? Did you feel peaceful or joyous?

Likewise, in daydreaming you may find yourself thinking about how an event in the future will unfold. This unfolding will happen according to what you **believe**, at the time, that the scenario of the event should occur. With that, pay close attention and you will recognize that the daydream you are experiencing (in your thinking) is either positive or negative. Are you having **good feelings or bad feelings** about and during this daydream? Let us look at this aspect of reflection more closely.

By **reflection** you will be able to notice that in your daily life, if you are having **mostly** good feelings and thoughts, then you are **being positive**. Therefore, if not, then the opposite is true about your thinking. Again, this exercise is very effective when you write your questions and your responses down on a piece of paper. Look at them. Do not become harsh with yourself if you do not like what you see. Do not judge yourself as good or bad. Seek to be aware and to understand how it is that you shape your life by the way that you think.

These thoughts literally do shape your life. They do shape your daily events, your circumstances, and your very existence. Your thoughts are yours. They are the only things over which you have total control. If they are negative in nature, and most people do have many, many of these thoughts, these negative thoughts will cause stress in your life. From this kind of thinking come failure, lack, illness, and the whole array of human emotions and conditions.

If your thoughts are positive in nature they will bring you love, joy, happiness, health, wealth, and positive self-expression.

As so many sages and successful people have stated, and in so many ways throughout history, "What you think about inside is what you get outside."

If you are **not** being successful in gaining and accomplishing your goals right now, if you are not getting what you want out of life right now, **Change Your Beliefs.** They are not working for you. How do you know if your beliefs are not working for you? Look around you. **Reflect** on what your life is like right now. Could it be better? Could your relationships be more harmonious? Do you have everything you want in your life in the way of love, money, good food, self-expression, friendships, travel, fun, and et cetera?

I am talking about, **you** taking **control** of your life! I am talking about you shaping and developing the lifestyle that you desire to have for yourself. Now if you apply this philosophy to your goal setting techniques, you **will** achieve your goals! And, how could you not?

Become the cause of the events in your life, instead of reacting to life's events.

Mixing the Mortar

So far in this book, let us say that I have been mixing the important elements needed to create the mortar, the cement, to lay down a foundation for change. Now, I am adding material to it to give it lasting strength. This is the Ancient Wisdom, knowledge from the past; tested by time and cultures throughout the world.

Ancient Wisdom

Can laws, statements or directives, that we call "Ancient Wisdom," be true for some people, but not for others? Or, can they be true sometimes but not other times? In itself, this statement scientifically says there is a problem here. Many will tell you that it is not because wisdom about a thing may be ancient, that makes it true. It could be a good rule of thumb or a guideline. If we call a statement a Universal Law and it does not apply to everyone, then how can it be a Universal Law?

The knowledge we have attained through science is a major factor of our evolution as a species. The intent of science is to prove or disprove that something of a discovery of knowledge is true or is no longer true. We prove a discovery's truth based on what humanity has learned by its accumulation of knowledge gained over the millennium.

Over time we have developed what is called The Scientific Method, which can also be used for analysis. In short, this method tells us that if you take certain steps in a certain fashion, the outcomes are of a certain end result (cause and effect; action and reaction). Thus, after a thorough examination of a discovery or a theory, we say, this is truth, or this is not. One of the greatest truths is **thinking creates**. Thinking is a cause!

So looked at scientifically, this ancient truth that "thinking," in and of its-self "creates," can be measured and it can be reproduced. We see accomplishment or achievement as a process, such as I think, and then I do. The process is really more like, because I think, IT becomes. This ability to think and create is one of the things we humans have in common with one another, and with the Universe. It is "The Power Within" and from whence we come.

As I said earlier, our predecessors have passed down to us this ancient wisdom of information for eons. I am writing to confirm that I have found their contents to be true. These Universal Laws work. They "really" work, and they are working for you and me always, even if we do not acknowledge them as true or existing. Understanding these few laws that I have out-lined in this book can, at the very least, help us to develop more peaceful lives. The law known as "Ask and you shall receive," has worked for millions of other people around the world to achieve whatsoever is their desire, so of course they must work for you and me as well. The actual law is, "Ask and it shall be given unto you according to your faith." You also have to be willing to receive, accept, and make room for its manifestation into your life, in order to fulfill the desired outcome.

Yes, one of the greatest truths handed down to us from generation after generation is: **By our thinking we create.** You can create the life of which you desire to live. Can you really ask to have more power than this? We can think, and therefore, we can create. We have the power to create our lives, our health, our careers, and our surroundings to be as we desire.

As I alluded to earlier, there are other factors involved in life. As other factors change the outcome of an experiment, so creating is thus complex. It sometimes seems that we do not have the control I have been talking about, but we do. There are no contradictions in Universal Laws. This requires a more in depth study of the **business of the Soul** and its relationship with the universe. These other factors do not negate the Universal Laws; though they are variables that can influences the outcomes. Facts, stories, and suggestions about the nature of Soul could indeed fill a book in itself. There is so much more to the miracle of life and our interactive relationship to God and the universe. Let me mention a couple of items for simplicity.

I will term this factor, "the maturity of the being" (you, me, us), our **readiness to understand and except**. For example, I was on this path to wonderment many years ago. Why would I step off this path? Why would I give up attaining my goals, "with ease and in perfect ways under Grace," after having already **sensed** the truth over twenty years ago? Why, after knowing, would I or anyone else, take the path of higher resistance, and even despair? I did just that. "When the student is **ready** the master will come." When you are ready to learn and accept, there is always someone or something to help you to understand. I guess in my case I just was not ready enough at the time. I am certain I did not really recognize the ramifications involved in my stepping off this path.

Here is another aspect or variable if you will. Take a look at this generation's Einstein, Stephen Hawkings. His biography was showcased on TV's "The Discovery Channel" some time ago. His theories, such as "Black Holes" in space, are highly respected throughout the world. He is a brilliant mind, by all definition, and in my opinion, and with an apparently wonderful sense of humor, yet physically he is almost entirely immobile. Why? **That is the business of his Soul.** He still thinks and achieves his goals, and makes great contributions to society.

The Soul's business is not all known to the great majority of us. I dare say that the few that do know are the likes of sages and saints, Buddha, Jesus, and Mohammed. I do not pretend to know.

Think of it as: With those of us who use a computer, I would venture to say that most of us know very little of its internal workings. However, learning and using its applications has changed our lives in countless and wonderful ways, and this is true around the world. You learn and then you practice using what you have learned until you say, "How did I ever live without it?" That is what was said about the telephone. That is what was said about the telephone answering machine, and so many of our other household conveniences. What will you say after you practice developing and reshaping your life, on purpose, with purpose?

The Soul's business is beyond wonder and imagination. But the point is, what is your life like today? Is your life in abundance of wonder and amazement? Do you see miracles? What have you created your life to be? If you are reading this material, it is in all probability, a signpost of your readiness for success, materialistically, and spiritually.

Think for your highest good and you will attain!

Fear versus Love

Fear

Fear has played a major role in our ability to survive since the beginnings of time, and to my knowledge this is true of all of the creatures on our planet. I believe you will find that most fears are false; brought on by mankind and our society, and by the human condition and conditioning. By that I mean, the perpetuation of false beliefs and superstitions handed down through generations. In our differing societies we are taught to fear certain things and certain events.

Dr. Murphy said appropriately in his book "The Power of the Subconscious Mind," innately we have two fears that lend to our survival, and they are, "…fear of noise and fear of falling." These two fears do help us. They are only intended as a precautionary psychological device to keep us aware of our surroundings and to help us to keep from being harmed. These two fears signal the "fight or flight" instinct innate in most, if not, all creatures throughout the world.

Let me list a few examples of fears that we bring about by our superstitions and negative thinking. I believe these to be man made fears. They are fear of: Success, lack, failure, God, the unknown, people, embarrassment, shame, guilt, animals, insects, a ladder, broken mirrors and of course, what is said to be one of the greatest fears of all, "public speaking." The list goes on and so does strife in the lives of mankind.

I know of no event in which for instance, a frog has ever attacked or bitten a human being, yet you yourself probably know of someone who is deathly afraid of frogs. I know a few people myself that are extremely afraid of these little creatures. How does this fear make any sense?

Your fears are real though, to the extent that you give them power, your power. Do not feed your fears with lies and more sub-vocal fuel. That will just strengthen them. If you give your fears fuel, they will control your life. Your fears can stop you cold. They will rob you of your God-given power to move forward in life. Moreover, in critical situations, your unwarranted fears can even get you killed.

"Face your fears and they will fall away" (Shinn). Wonderful growth awaits you when you judiciously, intelligently face your fears and overcome them. This also has been my experience.

Think Love

Think Love and you will grow in love's arms. Love is a very powerful energy.

That which you put your attention to is what you become. "What you think about you bring about." So think love.

Living in love is a choice you can make. The choices are, live in love or live in fear.

As far as humans are concerned, we, most all of us, live under both fear sponsored thoughts or love sponsored thoughts. Like a pendulum, we, our thoughts, swing back and forth and we live our lives under both conditions. I am talking about how we make the decisions we make. Some of our thoughts are sponsored by love and some are sponsored by fear. Much of our lives are reactionary in nature and based in fear. (Reactionary is still causal; cause necessitates effect.)

Here are some examples of fear sponsored thoughts and love sponsored thoughts. "If I succeed, people will expect much more from me. It would be awful to fail once I've succeeded." (Fear sponsored) "What if I tried and failed, I'll be too embarrassed to face my friends." (Fear sponsored) "If I don't meet this deadline I'll get fired." (Fear sponsored) "I love my job, I know how to do it and I can get it done on time." (Love sponsored) "I can't make this presentation, because they might laugh at me, because someone might ask me a question that I can't answer and I'll look foolish, because I'll choke up, because I'll be too nervous." (All fear sponsored) "I'll do the presentation and I'll get my message out. That's what is important to me." (Love sponsored) "Let me put together a wonderful dinner for my (significant other), then he or she will see that I love them and they will have to want to be with me." (Fear sponsored) "Let me make a wonderful dinner for that special person in my life because I want to show I care." (Love sponsored) Get the picture?

This is true about the way many people think about money as well. So many people, including people with good and stable incomes, show fears of spending as though they would not be able to replace the money they have used. This is "lack thinking," sponsored by fear.

To help yourself understand and become more aware of why you do the things you do and what is causing you to fear the situation you are faced with, you might ask yourself the questions "why" and "what" in the given situation. In other words, stop for a second and ask yourself: **What am I afraid of here in this situation? And, why am I afraid?**

Make time to reflect. For example: "I don't like Frank." "Why don't I like Frank?" "What am I afraid of?" "I don't like this or that." "Why? What am I afraid of?" "I can't…" "Why? What am I afraid of?" Wait for a quiet time when you can take the time to assess. This takes some practice, but it will help you to recognize your fears by looking at these situations at some point as they come up.

Think about this. Most of the time when we act out of love, we do not even think in the negative. I have not found a case in which one worries in the positive. How do you fear in the positive? "I worry about my children!" (Fear sponsored) Why worry? If you have taken care of your children's needs appropriately, then there is nothing left for you to worry.

Practice thinking in terms of love sponsored thoughts. God's love is energy in circulation. Do not short circuit the circulation by stopping it up and holding it back. Project love; give it out to those around you. You can even do this effectively by sending out love with your thoughts. Nobody even has to consciously know that you are doing it. Just send out thoughts of love. The next time you are stuck in traffic for instance, send love out to the people in the cars right next to you. They do not have to know.

Love is also a wonderful healing energy. It stems from God and it is always available. Love radiates from God to everyone who accepts it. Just keep it flowing. Accept it and pass it on to someone near or dear to you.

When we do something sponsored by love, we act on or react to a situation the best way we can. And, not because if we do not do this or that; well the consequences have a threat behind them, like lack, failure, embarrassment or something to cause worry. What I mean is that would be a, "We better do it or else" situation; a fear sponsored action or reaction to the situation.

Unconditional Love: God's Love

Think of it kind of like this: A baby is born to you or someone in your family. You have this sense of love for it. Moreover, this baby has done nothing to earn it. God does not wait for you to earn love. It is just there for you to accept it.

You too, have the capacity for unconditional love. Just practice it. Let people, and especially those who are closest to you, grow in your love unconditionally. This does not mean that you let people walk all over you and it does not mean you let your children run-a-muck. Discipline is love if it comes from love. It teaches your children self-discipline, orderly living, and safe living. I do not advocate corporal punishment. I do advocate teaching by example, with patience and understanding.

Unconditional love means, everyone is entitled to make their own mistakes and they are entitled to their own feelings. Everyone is entitled to grow at his or her own pace.

Unconditional love means, do not impose your priorities and beliefs on others, and it does not mean you would not love them if they do not do as you insist they do.

Unconditional love means, "I love you because I love you." Not because of the things you do, and not for the things you can give me.

Unconditional love is not just a matter of forgiveness, it is more like an understanding of the nature of things; God's nature. Study the nature of things by studying nature, physics, and metaphysics.

Since everyone is an expression of their soul, which is an expression of God, how can you but love them? How else can you return God's love to God?

Drench yourself in God's unconditional love and give it out, do not hold on to it. This never-ending supply of love will come back to you constantly just by accepting it. It has to, that is part of its nature.

Everyone is here to express themselves for the benefit of their soul's evolution. We do not condone actions of ill will, but we do not have to get wrapped up in someone else's game of life and trials either. Help someone when you can help, but do not do whatever it is, for him or her. Practice not judging people bad or good. Just keep the love thought in flow, unconditionally.

For those of us who need a reason to try anything, in this case I think you will find the return on investment is wondrous. Just for starters, you will be amazed at the amount of peace you will have in your life by the practice of giving out love unconditionally. By the way, God does not mind if you need a reason to get started. It's OK. You can silently bless everyone with love. God bless you!

Condemnation/Resentment

Condemnation, resentment, and victimization are also in the fear family. That is, you can relate each of them back to a fear. Without dragging this into a very long discussion, I would like to look at them separately from the previous discussion on fear.

What do you expect to receive from people and institutions when you condemn their efforts? When you condemn in others that which you would love to have for yourself, your subconscious looks at the condemnation as a "negation" of that which you say you would love to have for yourself. Therefore, it negates the thing you want, or worse, gives you the negative of what you want.

Consider this. You are doing daily affirmations. You are practicing developing your mental muscle in your beliefs and in faith, but your not creating for yourself this wonderful life promised to you. What are you really saying? Fact: Every thought you impress upon your subconscious mind causes it to start arranging things for you to receive, or it attracts to you that on which you put your attention. How do you feel about the success of others? Perhaps the success of your coworkers, friends, and classmates, leaves you **Feeling** a little resentful or envious. Maybe you feel a little victimized by being passed over for a promotion.

As a simple example, a coworker of yours gets a promotion, and you just cannot believe this person got it and you did not. You are even upset enough to have thoughts of how that person surely does not deserve the promotion as much as you do. "He got the promotion, but I didn't, and I'm more deserving, and I work harder than he does." With these thoughts you might just as well have said, "I really don't want success in my life." That is how your resentment or condemnation works against you. Therefore, you further reduce your chances of success coming to you any-time soon, and add one more frown wrinkle to your face to boot.

I am sure by now you would agree that these kinds of thoughts are negative in nature. I highly recommend that you be glad for your coworker and bless them. Bless them and their success, and you will confirm the same for yourself. At the very least, the blessing you send out will come back to you and bring you peace.

All thoughts affect your subconscious, positive as well as negative thoughts; especially those driven by the added power of feelings, such as love, sex, fear, anger, hate, and other emotions as well.

God

If you take water out of the ocean in a glass, you will hold exactly what the ocean is, in that glass, but it is not the ocean. The ocean is vastly greater. I am and you are, an expression of God. We are that which he is, but like the ocean, He is so much more.

I believe the reason that man, as it has been said, has always created a God, could be that most of us throughout the ages intuitively sensed something much greater than that which we are.

This is how I look at my relationship to God. I am an expression of God. Therefore, I have the same qualities as God has. But I am much smaller in scope than is God. God is like this math configuration, 3=1+1. This numerical example means that the whole is greater than the sum of its parts. All of us added together are not all that God is. Everything you have ever created does not add up to all of who you are. Would you not agree that there is always more of you than all of what you have accomplished in life?

I have written this book to confirm from my experiences that these teachings do manifest success, abundance, happiness, joy, miracles, and wonders beyond our imaginations, as they have for me. Please understand that the subject of God is based on my beliefs, which are based on what I have learned form different teachers and various studies that I have made. My beliefs about God are from my observations and sensations, which are perfect for me. This section is different in that I, other than what I have stated, personally know nothing about God. I would be guessing or lying if I said I did know.

Many philosophers, far more knowledgeable than myself, say that God is unknowable. This is not hard for me to believe. Like the sub-atomic particles of quantum physics whose trace effects we can observe, we give names to them, but they in themselves cannot be seen or known. However, they do exist, just as surely as does God.

Thanks to God, in the universe there exists every opportunity for expression. As a co-creator with God, "you" get to decide whether you will express the negative or the positive aspect of life in your life. This is <u>your</u> choice!

Here is another aspect that is easy for me to believe. God is unknowable, know yourself, which you can do, and therefore, you can know His expression; His Trace evidence. Know yourself and you can also know others, and with that, now you can know more of God by His countless expressions.

"From nothing come ten thousand things." I always thought this was a wonderful interpretation of a piece from *The Tao Teh Ching*, another writing passed down to us from ancient times referring to "The Beginning."

"In The Beginning" is a constant cycle. Looking at this cycle it is just like, **you have a thought.** You crave its manifestation into your life. It is your desire to have this thing and you are grateful knowing it has already come to pass. You have faith in its manifestation, because you have already created it in your thoughts, so it does already exist in its fullness on that level. And, through your subconscious mind, Infinite Intelligence brings it about for you to have in your physical reality. Once again, your thoughts are followed by energy and they bring matter together to create. This is the cycle. Before the thought there was nothing, and then there was the thought; the thought brought about existence and the wonders never ceased.

Everything ever built on this planet and in this universe began with a thought. Be it a home, a bridge or a business, everything is a thought first. Where do your thoughts come from?

God is unknowable, but it is easy to see His trace evidence. His expression is everywhere.

Here is one more thing about God I have learned that makes sense for me. Which for me showed me answers to the questions I have had about pain and suffering in the human condition.

First of all, God does not cause pain and suffering, we in our human personalities do. Our negative mental imaginings do that for us and to us. Everything in existence is an expression of God, from His imagination. Therefore, so is every single person everywhere, made in His image. Therefore too, God punishes no one. That would be like God punishing God. How would that make any sense?

That which you put your attention on is what comes about for you. As you practice what you have learned about taking responsibility for your life, your thoughts, and the powers of positive thought, you can prove this for yourself. Put your attention on right thinking, thoughts of a virtuous nature. Put your attention on happy and positive thoughts, and see if your life flows in those directions. Try it and prove it for yourself, because this "way" of "being" is reproducible and measurable. That is what makes it scientific.

"All things will be done unto you according to your faith." Put your attention on thoughts of loss, pain, sorrow, and then in all probability, at the very least, you will attract stressful situations in your life.

God did create our amazing system with duality built in it. If there was no dark, how could we know light? If it were not for the beauty in the color of black, how would we see the beauty of the stars? If there was not negative, how could we know positive? If there was no sadness, could we know joy? If there were no you, how could I even begin to know me? Why would I? Moreover, how could I know that I exist? We are reflections of each other. Where would I be, if there were no you?

God may be unknowable, but His face is in everyone you meet. Everything is, and we are, Traces of God's existence. There is only God and love. The opposite of love is fear. Fear can be overcome because it is false, but how do you overcome love? You cannot. So, in reality, there is only God and love.

Be Grateful

Always show thanks. Saying thanks to God, Infinite Intelligence, your Higher Power, or Yourself, shows appreciation and acknowledgment.

You cannot effectively give something to someone who has everything. I am sure that many of us have experienced the frustration of buying a gift for someone who seems to have everything. You want to show them you love them or that you care about them, or maybe you just want to stay on their good side. You do this for relatives, friends, acquaintances, bosses, and clients too; do you not? Giving gifts is an expression of appreciation and acknowledgment. Now you can practice expressing appreciation and acknowledgement to yourself, and to any Higher Power in which you believe.

My personal belief, that which I grew up with, is a belief in a single God, the creator of all that is. The way that I believe, that is, my concept of God has change considerably from the concept I grew-up with in my culture.

Just the same I could not understand why a God might want my thanks. He has everything and to top it off, I believed, it does not matter to Him what I do, how I live, or what I believe. He has it all. Why would He care if I gave thanks to Him?

For myself, I found that the answer is acknowledgment that He exists, that I exist because He exists. In His unconditional love, He has always known that I would, and you would, someday seek Him. It took me a long time to get something tangible to understand this, and the answer, like all answers, was with me forever. I found it in a simple thing like having someone say, "thank you" to me for holding a door open for them; for another person. This is what opened my eyes to this question. That I received acknowledgment from another person that I exist, that I have meaning, that I am.

I was taught that it is one of those polite things you do, holding open a door for someone, just as it is as polite to say thank you to someone for doing the same for me. On reflection one day, I realized I would feel a little irritated when I would hold a door opened for someone and they did not acknowledge me. I would always shrug it off, but I would always feel the irritation every time this happened. When someone would say, "thank you," I did not become elated, or overwhelmed with joy. It was just nice for me that someone would give me a simple thanks or nodded their head. You know, acknowledgment, thank you. "I recognize you and your kindness to me." Maybe that is all my God wants from me. Maybe it means more than that.

Just like with relatives, friends, your boss, and clients, you are saying, "I want to have and maintain a harmonious relationship of giving and receiving between us." Moreover, that is what you get in return! Let me state it for clarity. You get more of what you give and more than what you gave. The return on giving comes back to you on many levels.

Always show thanks. Give thanks! Give thanks to God. Give your thanks to one of the many expressions of God. It does not make you subservient; it makes you "great-full!"

Giving and Receiving

Always practice *judicious thinking*. Be pensive, reflective and maintain a kind attitude.

Giving and receiving is the current of life; the currency. In addition, understand that money is the happy medium that we use as currency. If you do not have a wonderful relationship with money, then develop one. "Practice being part of the flow." Do not bottle up the flow of current. Be part of it.

You get nothing for nothing. Give nothing and you receive nothing.

You do have plenty to give and yet, for some people that sub-vocal voice of fear says, "I lack, I have nothing to give." There are those who honestly believe this, because of fears that they have developed over the years! Some people, due to fear of loss, or their fear of lack, do not even recognize that they take, hoard, and hold on to whatever they receive. There are those too, who for a lot of reasons, such as childhood rearing, religious teachings, et cetera, give well but they do not receive well. They know how to say thank you, but they just do not think they deserve to receive.

You would serve yourself well do to do both, give and receive, and be part of the current. Give unconditionally and receive unconditionally. To receive, you only need to accept. Accept with thanks. Give with an open heart; receive with an open heart, open mind, and open arms. Then, give some more. Judiciously give what you can when you can and without guilt, resentment or concern. Train yourself, if you must, to give just because. Give your time, your love and your attention. Give your knowledge, your smile, and your feelings. And YES, give your money too. It is all a part of the current of life. Give all things when it feels right to do so.

The universe is abundant and is always supplying. All of these things you possess come from the universe, and they are all energies. Take them in and give them out, and in doing so, you become a conduit through which the Universe flows never ending. When you practice giving, you will find that you are never without; what a wonder your life becomes.

Let me add this quote from Mother Teresa. "We cannot show our love for God whom we cannot see and who is in need of nothing except by loving and serving our neighbour whom we see and love as God's child" (E. LeJoly and J. Chaliha).

Study

Do not waste your very precious time on Earth. How can you know if you are on the right path in life? You can know by doing the things you love doing for fun, or in your career. Where you put your attention, what you focus on, that is what you bring forth into your life.

In order that I could have what I hoped would be a fun and interesting career, I studied what I thought I would enjoy doing.

When I was a younger man I studied to be an aircraft mechanic, which I really enjoyed doing. I was an aircraft mechanic for about twenty years. When that career ended for me, I studied to be a realtor and I studied business, which I found I enjoyed even more. Later, because of my involvement in community service and working with elementary school children, I became very interested in teaching. So I studied that, and that is what I did for a few years as well, and with great pleasure.

Study what you are interested in learning. Study that which will enhance your opportunities to achieve your goals. Study that which will enable you to do your job better in whatever you are doing now in life.

We know that some of the greatest men that ever walked the earth had no formal education. We know too, that some of the greatest men in history had extensive educations. What they seemed to have had very much in common was a desire to succeed, and that they practiced using what they had learned to enhance their lives, and ours.

Academics studies are important. Formal or informal studies are important. What you learn from others gives you the basis for self-expression. You learn from someone else so you can make the information your own and then you express yourself even better.

Study your relationship with the universe and with God. It would be advisable to make time to study the Universal Laws; the Metaphysical Laws. You will find peace and you will function better in society along with creating a better life for yourself. The reasons for studying Metaphysical Laws are the same reasons we study physical laws. To know the laws to better understand how things work, so that we may live more harmoniously within our realm; to have less strife and more conveniences. All in all, we study these laws so that we can develop a better way of life.

Let us begin with the fact that there are, as we call them, Universal Laws. These are like the laws of physics. In fact, they include the laws of physics. Though the laws of physics are observations made on things, acts, and events in and of the physical world in which we live, we can say basically, that the same is true for Universal Laws. The physical laws just seem more tangible, whereas the term "Universal Laws," is used mostly when discussing the metaphysical realm.

Let us look at physical laws first. The study of physical laws has made our lives easier and more carefree. Over the millennium, through the study of physics, or physical science, we have come to know much more about our physical universe, which of course includes the galaxy in which we live.

So the study of physics, we can say, is a scientific method of searching for that which is true about the nature of life and our relationship to, or with everything else. It is the quest for knowledge through close observation of what we perceive as our physical universe through our five senses.

Through close observation, or if you prefer the use of the term "study," of a certain action we note a certain re-action. And with that, if we create certain conditions, we cause certain outcomes to come to pass. Therefore, through the study of the laws of physical science, we have also found that we can learn to accurately predict the outcome, or probable outcome, through a course of action.

Based on the study of these physical laws, we have developed medical techniques to help us to live longer and healthier. We have at our disposal, fairly easy access to a variety of medicines and drugs. We have overcome so many of the diseases that plagued our forefathers not so very long ago.

For example: We can predict outcomes based on the observation of activities of chemicals, to produce medicines, of ingredients, to create wonderful tasting foods, and of weather patterns, to forecast weather, just to mention a few areas.

Through the study of physical science, we have the advent of household appliances and gadgets. Now our lives are so much more convenient than even fifty years ago, not to mention the changes that have occurred in our lives from 100 years ago. These gadgets could only have come into being by our expanded imagination, and of course, due to the study of physical laws. It is all based on close observation of action and reaction, cause and effect, to determine what is true about a thing or event. This is absolutely true in metaphysical Universal Laws as well.

Ok, getting back to metaphysics and Universal Laws. They are not just some term that we give to things unexplainable that just happen to work and then we pass it off as a New Age term.

I have nothing against New Age. Many of the books I have enjoyed are stored in the New Age section of the bookstore. Let me explain what I meant. Unfortunately, and I think that primarily because of the way bookstores stock their bookshelves, New Age has come to encompass everything from dragons and vampires to Tarot, UFOs, Soul, and God. Since we use the term "Universal Laws" often in metaphysics and books of New Age, it gives some the impression that a Universal Laws have less value and are less scientific in meaning, than principles expressed in physical laws. Nothing can be further from the truth. By the way, and I think you will agree, New Age was originally intended as an awareness of a new way to study our relationship to the self, to God, and spiritualism.

Universal Laws pertain to the study of the physical as well as the metaphysical realm. Metaphysical is all encompassing, meaning it includes that which is physical as well. It is the realm of thought. The important thing to remember is that it means, a Universal Law is always true for everyone and not true just sometimes, as in, a rule of thumb.

So, if "Ask and you shall receive" is a Universal Law, then it is true for everyone.

First of all, and factually, whatever you ask for, even once, can manifest itself into your physical realty. Here is the gist of it. By this Universal Law we create our physical world to be as we believe it to be. By that I mean, as individuals we use the Universal Laws of Cause and Effect along with the law that states "Ask and you shall receive" (which pertains to the Law of Attraction), to create our lives including our health, career, financial status, living conditions, et cetera. That said; the following is the reason and the mechanisms of how and why this works. **Thought creates.** This too, is a Universal Law.

Definitions

Define the tools of thought that create. Define the words in this section for yourself. Understand the nature of their true power. It is very important that you become pro-active in your own personal growth, and in finding out who you really are.

Let me get you started. All of these words are followed by energy. Your desire to attain and accomplish, sets everything else in motion depending on the strength of your desire. Develop for yourself a strong sense of desire. The rest of these words or expressions, in essence, create more energy to help you to demonstrate or accomplish your goals. Your subconscious mind is always there with you, listening, and ready to help you to attain your desires.

Thought, Desire, Purpose, Intention, Emotion, Belief, Faith, and Action

Your Word is Your Wand (Florence Scovel-Shinn). Practice asking, give thanks for everything and become aware that you do create. Life is what you make it to be.

Thought: "What you think about you bring about." This is the beginning, where everything starts. Your desires come from your imagination, your thoughts. Thoughts are symbols and images within you that have meaning to you. When you have a thought, an idea that motivates you into action, we generally identify this as a desire. Energy follows thought, which brings matter together to form reality.

Desire: A will to have or to accomplish. Develop a strong desire for whatever you *wish* to have and create a need for it. Desire will inspire your imagination (imaging) further, which greatly enhances the attainment of your goals. Create a strong desire, and you will always receive what you need, and to create a space for in your life.

Purpose: Your life is purposeful. You are an important part of "All That Is." You add to your society's good. Develop goals and seek to accomplish them, on purpose, with purpose. Wake up everyday with a purpose in mind. Even your everyday "Honey Do" list is purposeful and can lend to the feeling of accomplishment.

Intention: Intend for good and you will be surrounded by good. Caution: The opposite is also true. Intention can be a very strong idea and it can also lead to, or support an emotion.

Emotion: Your subconscious mind, Higher-self, Soul, Infinite Intelligence, is always listening to you. Emotion impacts and impresses it greatly to carry out your desires. Regardless of whether the emotion is fear based or love based, they are both powerful driving forces. Though as I have stated, fear is false, it can be felt as real to you and therefore, it can continue to be a strong driving force in your life.

Belief: Beliefs are the thoughts and things you accept to be true. You can develop the belief in yourself that your desires will be manifest. Realize also that some things take time to develop.

Faith: Create in yourself a knowing and an expectation. "…done unto you according to your faith," means you will receive what you ask for based on the depth of your faith, your expectation to receive. Even those tiny negating thoughts that creep in and disrupt your positive affirmations, without your total awareness, will defuse the fullness of your desire to something less than what you have asked. Practice asking. Just keep affirming with undaunted expectation. Your faith will greatly determine the outcome of your desire. Like the great oak tree, from a tiny seed it becomes. So it is that your thoughts and desires take time to become.

Action: Do your part. "Fake it 'til you make it." Portray in you that whom you desire to become. Impress your subconscious mind. In reality; "God helps those who help themselves." And very important, if you want to impress your subconscious with your desire to attain, "Plan your work-Work your plan," with faith not with pressure. If you fine that you must push to accomplish a task, that could mean there is pressure due to resistance, and that means there is not ease. This is a good indication that it is time to reassess yourself, your plan, and maybe even your goal. That said, even if you are doing things incorrectly, the fact that you are "doing" means that you are focused on your desire to achieve an end result, and you will achieve that desired end result.

Order

Before I go on to discuss order and its relationship to health, I would like to remind you that all end results, whether we consider them to be good or bad, are caused by prior conditions and circumstances. So this certainly includes the state of your health as well. Even when we say that some things not know to us and are the business of the Soul, the cause of things on this plane of existence is also caused by prior conditions and circumstances.

Order is that which holds the universe in perfect running condition. Order causes predictability and stability. Just look at our solar system as an example of billions of years of order.

All organizations that function with ease are based on order. Your body is an organism, an organization, created and based on order, composed of trillions of cells brought together by an idea. Each cell in your body is meant to work in harmony with one another. This organism, your body, is reliant on you, your conscious self, to help maintain this order with healthy, positive thinking habits.

Let me make yet another very long story a little shorter for our purpose in this book. Order affords ease of operation. Dis-order causes disease. Dis-ease causes disease, which when left unchecked, un-cared for, can and will, cause mental and physical stress. We know stress causes emotional discomfort and physical illness. In addition, we know that great amounts of debilitating diseases are brought on by habitual negative thinking. Most all disciplines of science will attest to this fact. This brings us back to the fact that your thoughts cause the conditions and circumstances of your life; that includes the state of your health, be it good health or poor health. If you were not aware, you now know that order brings about harmony and disorder causes stress. Stress, in turn, brings about a whole range of illnesses.

Healing

When you are ill there is something in your life that is out of balance; something is out of order. Healing is based on reordering, restructuring, and recreating those parts of you, those aspects of you that are out of balance. To begin the healing processes, first ask your subconscious mind to heal you. Have faith. Know that your subconscious, your Higher Self is healing and rapidly re-creating healthy new cells for you, because that is what it does, and because you asked for the healing.

You believed your mother when after you skinned your knee, and she cleaned it up, she said, "You'll be alright now." Shortly thereafter, you were back to playing and did not even notice the pain (nor the healing). It was thus so, because you believed.

In the healing process, it is very important that you do that which is necessary. "God helps those who help themselves." You must actively participate in the healing process. With your intelligent cooperation and faith, you will be healed. Recognize and accept that through you, people help you to heal. Seek medical attention. Recognize also, that nature helps you to heal. Seek to take-in nutrients, some sunshine, and fresh air.

To help you increase the flow of oxygen and blood throughout your body to affect healing, you might practice relaxation techniques or meditation. Move your body with ease and care, as much as possible, and as soon as possible.

To heal an affliction, it must materialize; it must be brought to the surface to your conscious awareness. It must be brought to your attention and recognized for what the affliction is. This disease just wants and needs to be dealt with properly. Do not commiserate or agonize over it. You will only encourage it to stick around; you will help to prolong the illness, injury, or affliction. Think and take judicious action.

The healing begins, and the reordering begins, when a disorder occurs and is recognized.

I have made this following statement a part of my daily affirmations. You may wish to make it your own as well. "Minute-by-minute, day-by-day, my Father brings me closer-and-closer to perfect health in body and in mind."

A Strong Foundation

We have the mortar and we have added the lasting strength. Now we set the iron rods in place to secure a strong foundation upon which to build our lives.

Create Balance in Your Life

As with any structure you wish to build, you always want to have a good sturdy foundation upon which to build. The tallest of buildings are balanced on well thought out foundations. This is also true with any long lasting business, and it is as necessary for the individual person as well.

Several years ago I learned that if I was not enjoying my life I had to look at what I was doing, or maybe not doing. Our life's foundation starts with personal care on which to place our philosophy of life.

There are four aspects fundamental to building a strong, healthy foundation and creating balance in your life. They are: **Creativity, Play, Diet and Rest.** I will define them and afterward you can redefine them for yourself should you feel the need.

Creativity is what you do, your work or your hobbies. It is that which comes from you; the things you do that give you the feeling of satisfaction and of accomplishment. If you ignore this aspect of your being, in all probability through boredom or depression, it may slowly cause your end. This is because you are born a creative being and acting less than that causes so many negative repercussions that its lack can lead to illness and death.

Play is a wonderful release of energy and expression. Play games. Play for the physical exercise. Dance or go swimming. Be involved in sports and challenges. Do it for the fun of it, and not just for the competition. "It's not winning that is important; it's how you play the game." Take time to make the time for play, and be social.

Again, if you ignore this aspect of your being, in all probability through boredom, depression, and the feeling of rejection, even when the rejection is brought on by yourself, this too, may slowly cause your end. This is because you are born to be a socially active being searching for unity with others. Not participating in life may leave you feeling left out and unwanted. Acting as less than a social being can cause so many negative repercussions which can lead to illness and death.

Diet is just that which you are accustom to eating. Eating is a process by which we derive vitamins and nutrients to vitalize our bodies. We can eat and manage to sustain our lives by eating almost anything. Sustaining and being in good health are not necessarily the same thing. Eat that which you can best afford and that is most nutritious.

Diet is a very important aspect of life. Many people do not treat this aspect with much respect. Even the producers of foods are gathering to market food, such as fruits and vegetables, before they are mature enough to supply all the nutrients that they otherwise may have supplied our bodies.

When it comes to the aspect of diet, take the time to treat your body as well as you can. Feed your body food that it can best process and derive the nutrients it needs. Like the other aspects necessary to create a balanced and strong foundation, the lack of care about your diet, in all probability, will cause your end. This too, when ignored, causes so many negative repercussions that can lead to illness and death.

There has always been research available pointing to what seems to be the fact that being a vegetarian, or eating a primarily vegetarian diet, is healthier for the human body then diets low in fruits and vegetables. It is my personal belief and from my experience on the whole that this is correct. I personally feel better and more active when I do not eat meats, or when I have very little meat with a meal.

As was confirmed for me at a lecture I went to given by Anthony J. Fisichella; in the evolutionary food chain, that which is least spiritually evolved is easer for your body to digest. Because vegetation is of a nature of lower awareness than animals are, vegetation is easier to digest.

Note: As you may know, being a vegetarian, in and of itself, does not make you more spiritually evolved.

Think for a moment of how blessed we are when it comes to buying or making a simple sandwich. Is it not something of a miracle when you consider the large amount of people and resources involved? Would this not also apply to the people living in rural areas, as they too shop for groceries? It has become my belief that in the final analysis, blessing the foods you take into your being does seem to help the body to digest that food more effectively.

So before eating your meal, take the time to think of the many people that are involved in making the simple act of buying or making a sandwich possible for you. Bless them as well as the foods you put into your body.

Rest comes in many forms. Rest is what we do to cause the body to feel refreshed and regenerated.

Let me start with an extreme example. For our purpose let us call true rest an ultimate and attainable condition of the body. True rest is found when there is no tension in any of the muscles in your body; when the respiratory system is at minimal operation, and oxygen and blood are flowing with great ease. When your body is totally relaxed and nothing in your body is moving, other than the transmission of blood caring nutrients and oxygen to various parts of the body to revitalize and energize each of its cells, then we can say you have attained true and ultimate rest.

Thinking can interrupt true rest, because it does cause tension in the physical body. For example, fearful thoughts, and even happy thoughts, cause muscles in certain areas of the body to tense. This, in turn, restricts the flow of energy throughout the body and reduces the opportunity for true rest.

Sleep, meditation, and relaxation techniques, are the predominant methods of resting your body and your mind. To some extent you can even find rest in a peaceful stroll in the park or sitting along a bank of a stream of water or on a shoreline. Just sit quietly for a few minute each day anywhere that you are and rest. The excessive loss of rest may cause so many negative repercussions that it can lead to illness and death as well.

Some of us as children missed out on some of these aspects of life as we grew-up. But that is in the past; balance your life in the now. Start with these all-important fundamentals. If you are not attending to these areas of your life, reassess and recreate the balance in your life; in your fundamental foundation. Your foundation needs these four major aspects: **Creativity, Play, Diet and Rest**, because they will help you to develop an even-tempered attitude upon which to build your life. Your well-being is dependent upon you incorporating these aspects into your life properly.

Law of Attraction

Remember always: "What you think about you bring about," and it does not matter whether your thoughts and/or actions, are for good or not for good, for a positive or for a negative purpose. Your thoughts are followed by energy and thoughts are cause; cause necessitates effect.

The following are aspects of the Law of Attraction:
* Like attracts like.
* What you radiate yourself to be is who and what you will attract into your life.
* You attract that which you portray.
* You get in kind what you give.
* Thinking and doing always get results…Action/Reaction, Cause and Effect.
* Those with whom you associate are reflections of who you are. You have attracted these people into your life.

* You are always in communication with your subconscious mind, so impress it with thoughts and deeds that will attract to you what you really desire.

Reflect often on what you think about and how you are thinking. Your thinking habit is your way of life, literally speaking. How you perceive everyone and everything to be is a reflection of you. Moreover, it is a very good indicator of your habit thinking.

Habit Thinking

You will almost always fall into a habit of some sort. Choose healthy habits.

Your way of life is always based on the thinking habits you have developed throughout your life. In other words, your daily life activities are a reflection of your thinking habits.

Example: What is the first thing you do when you get up in the morning, and then the next thing you do, and the next; throughout your day? Even the most mundane things you do (actions) are based on the way you think things should happen in your life's daily routine. This is true for every aspect in your life. You can choose to make changes in your life by changing your thinking. After all, it is your mind, and **your mind is the only thing over which you can have total control.**

Train your thoughts to be on that which is for your highest good. Impress your subconscious mind with these thoughts by action and affirmations daily; morning, noon, and night. Gain control over your life by taking control of your mind and purposely being the cause of the things that are going on in your life based on your new thinking habits.

Give your attention to thoughts of love, peace, health, wealth, harmonious relationship, and perfect self-expression. Put your attention on your role in your community and your life will change because your habit thinking is changing.

Law of Change

Change occurs because it must. Change is evolution, and with time, everything and everyone evolves (changes) in consciousness and in spirit.

People change; conditions change. To read this book, to read any material, causes active change in you.

As I change all conditions change; throughout the world, throughout the universe. We are connected to everything, so everything must change as well. As I improve myself, all things are improved. Did things change around the world after Edison developed the light bulb? Did things change around the world after Marconi developed audio communications, the radio? Furthermore, what about each individual who added to bringing in the advent of the personal computer; did they cause change in the world?

What about you here, at this point in your life? The things you do or do not do also affect the world. We are involved in a world market. What you buy or do not buy will affect someone's economy somewhere in the world, maybe more subtly than some major scientific discovery, but without doubt it will have an effect.

Example: The new car you buy in your city will probably put money in the pockets of families all around the world. Think of it! Have you not affected a change in your life by buying a new car? So, as you change all conditions change, around the world.

As the tiny pebble is dropped into a pond that causes ripples to find their way to the shorelines in the calmest of waters, you too, affect the world and the universe by your growth, or your stagnation. Make it your goal to create waves of abundance. That is your birthright.

Note: Physical science and metaphysical science both agree. Matter cannot be destroyed, it can only be changed. Likewise, you do not lose anything, you do not die and cease to exist; you just change form. Like water can be changed into an ice cube or changed into steam, it is still H_2O. It is still water, but it just changed forms. Things change because they must.

Understand that although you may want the best for someone close to you, you cannot change someone else's thinking for them. You see that someone you care about lives in lack and you want him or her to live better; that necessitates a change of thinking habit on his or her part.

Let us again use money as an example. Having an abundance of money necessitates a change of mind and a change of attitude in a person who lacks. First of all, lack of money comes from a "lack" attitude. Often this lack attitude is caused by a habit thinking of worry of not having enough. That kind of thinking in itself causes the lack of money. Once you make the change of thinking to abundance, and abundance becomes your habit thinking, then that is what you will have. Without the change in thinking, it does not happen. The change in thinking is a personal choice which stems from a change in personal belief. So you can be an example to those you care about, but you cannot change their thinking for them.

Here is another money example: You come into a lot of money; let us say a million dollars. There is an old adage that says, "You can receive a million dollars, but if you don't become a millionaire, you don't get to keep the million dollars." This means if you do not change your mind, if you do not think like a person of money, you will probably miss use it, and then you will lose the money that you suddenly received. That is why so many winners of the lottery are millionaires one year and lose everything, and then some, the next year. In order to be able to keep the money, that person must become a more abundant and responsible thinker. But remember, you cannot change someone's mind for them.

Note: As we learn to change our thinking and grow, and our lives become richer and more peaceful, we may develop a tendency to want others to benefit from what we have learned, and some will benefit. We naturally want the people closest to us to do well and progress through life with ease. By what I have stated earlier, again and again, you should understand that you cannot make someone else's life for them. You can change your mind and lead your life. You can be a role-model for those you care about and others as well, but you cannot change someone's life for them. They "gotta wanna" change it for themselves.

To affect changes in their lives, they have to be willing to make the changes in there "beliefs, attitude, and behavior" for themselves. They have to make the effort to change their own mind.

Destiny/ Predestined

Two people meet and develop a wonderful relationship. "It was meant to be." The relationship breaks down and the relationship is dissolved. "It was meant to be."

You go on vacation to another country and find that there you meet a person from your hometown. By the time you arrive back to your hometown you have become great friends. "It was meant to be."

You go to school to become a doctor, because this is what was expected of you in your family. So, "It was meant to be." But you found that something was missing in your life. Perhaps you have always loved the piano, and you play it so well. You give up your medical practice, go into music and fine that you do pretty well (financially). So, "It was meant to be."

Two people meet and learn something they feel was really important to each of them from one another, and then they go their own separate ways. "It was meant to be."

So are things predestined? Would you expect that the phrase "meant to be" negates free will? Did I mention that there are no accidents? Things are not always as they seem. Did I mention that your higher-self does everything to bring about whatever you have asked for into your life? "Ask and you shall receive." "What you think about, you bring about." Therefore, and because you asked at some point in the past, it has to be, and in that way yes, "it was meant to be." It is your right as co-creator to have what you will.

Bear with me. This may take some explaining. Let us go back to cause and effect and look at it one more time.

Certain end results always happen due to certain prior conditions and circumstances. If you plant and nurture a tomato seed, you do not get a pine tree. If you follow all of the necessary steps and apply the ingredients that it takes to bake a chocolate cake, then you will not get vanilla pudding. So too, if you want a college diploma, it is your desire, and if you successfully jump through all of the hoops that college requires, then you get a college diploma. Someone else has already set up the steps that you agreed to follow, though you still asked for it.

The end results are predestined based on the prior conditions YOU created, along with the Creator, which is primary cause. In that way, of course, and based on prior conditions and circumstances, the end result is always "meant to be."

With people and relationships the answer is not as easy to see. We are destined to get what we ask for, period! Again, there are no accidents. Universal Laws are universal because they are impersonal and are true for all of us. Things have to come about as they should, based on what we want and based on our "beliefs, attitude, and behavior." (Moreover, as you may recall, based on our daily habit).

Most often, the reason things do not occur as we would like to have them occur, is because of the variable of adding another thought, positive or negative, to our claim (affirmation or prayer).

When it comes to relationships with other people specifically, "we get what we ask for," "but" there has to be agreement between the people involved in the relationship, because we get what we ask for as individuals (as well as what we ask for as a group). There needs to be a commonality in the thinking between the individuals in the relationship; things like mutual trust, mutual interests, mutual admiration, and et cetera.

Short example: Take two people in a committed relationship and one of the people no longer desires the other. Because of the change in the thinking (desire) of one of the people in the relationship, there maybe an array of outcomes from peaceful to violent. Of course what must follow, in most cases, would seem to mean an end to that relationship.

The fact is things are predestined to happen based on the prior conditions and circumstances to an event or to the end result. As in the example, even in relationships, the prior conditions and circumstances of the relationships are created by the individuals in the relationship. Thus, their individual thinking will cause cohesion or separation of the union.

Does not the phrase "It was meant to be" relieve us of our responsibilities? How can that be? Again, if it were true, then the phrase "It was meant to be" would negate free will.

Regardless of the event or relationship, **you do have free will and control over your life, because you have control over your thoughts, and by that, to a great extent, you do have control over your destiny.**

Be Quiet

"Be still…" and learn about who you really are.

By paying attention to what you think about and what kinds of thoughts you are indulging in, you can become aware so that you can make the necessary changes in your thinking for your higher good, and toward a better life. Relaxation techniques and meditation greatly help to accelerate this process. The greatest benefits I can think of that are brought about from these practices are the feeling of peace and release of negative thinking. At the higher end, when you become proficient and at peace with your **Self**, this is where communion takes place. Until then, your subconscious is still listening anyway.

If you become involved and practice techniques of relaxation or meditation, eventually you will find many physical benefits as well. It does take time, but you do not have to wait until you have mastered these techniques to derive their benefits. I feel that these exercises are well worth the effort.

Becoming still means, taking conscious control to put at ease every muscle in your body. Even early on, as you begin practicing being still or relaxation techniques, your mind may or may not get distracted by daydreams or thoughts, positive or negative. This is because of the factor of concentration. That is, concentration on relaxing each muscle as you start from head to toe, or vice versa, does not give your mind much of a chance to wonder about other things. It may be more difficult to put into practice than it sounds, but as I said, the physical effects alone are worth the effort.

As you become proficient with the physical aspect of being still, that is when your mind again starts to pay attention to the numerous thoughts that come into your awareness. This is where, in my opinion, the challenge really begins in quieting the mind. As you will notice, these thoughts of yours will come into your mind to be examined. The trick is to not let them hold your attention, but rather to let them come and go. The idea in meditation is to avoid even as much as an acknowledgment that these thoughts are there for you to give your attention. Then, a time will come when this barrage of thoughts will diminish.

There is a quite space between your thoughts. This quiet space is where you will want to place your attention. This is where the peace is. This is "being still." This is what is really meant by the phrase, "Clear your mind." The thoughts will keep coming. If you do not grab on to one, they will keep going, and you will gently place yourself back in between the thoughts where the peace is.

Scientists call this quite space the Alpha state, named for the Alpha brain waves, a very relaxed state of mind. We are said to reach or be in this state at twilight sleep. That is the conscious space you are in just before falling asleep or upon wakening. In meditation, your purpose is to be consciously aware of this state and then start to learn about who you really are. (See the meditation technique at the end of this book)

When you are able to be quiet you are better able to listen and accept the information and communication that comes to you. If you want to learn anything, then for a thing to be learned you must understand it. So be quiet and become aware. Give a thing your attention and you gain understanding of it.

Learning comes to you, which is to say to your conscious mind, through your five senses and by being quiet. It also comes to you from inside of you when you are quiet.

"Seek first to understand and then to be understood." Read Stephen Covey, he conveys this thought wonderfully.

How do you gain the knowledge of the needs of your clients, customers, employees, employer, friends, and relatives? Be quiet and listen. Even when you are sure you know the answer you want to respond with, practice listening, and be quiet. You cannot listen if you are talking, you must be quiet.

In sales, the opposite of being quiet is known as over selling, which may cause you to lose a deal. For example: You have someone sold on a product or service that you are offering in the first five minutes of your presentation. Sometimes we get so wrapped up in expressing ourselves, because we sound so good, because we feel so good, and because we know we are about to wrap-up an important deal, we forget to be quite and just close the deal. You can see that the buyer is sold, and then you just keep on rattling. Suddenly you have brought up a question of concern in the buyer's mind that was not even there to begin with, and you lose the deal. Be quiet and listen.

If you are talking or writing, you are not listening with your full attention. Moreover, people, your associates, and your loved ones, will notice. They may even think you are not interested in them. Then, what have you got? Be quiet and listen.

You

Seek first the kingdom of heaven, which is your subconscious mind, and then all things are attainable, in harmony with the Universe.

You are an expression of God, your Higher Power, your Soul, and your Subconscious mind. This is true about each and every one of us.

With reflection, you may recognize that you have all the necessary tools to make of your life what you want it to be. You have always had all that you need to create the life that you want. You are an expression of God. What greater gift is there in life?

Bring your conscious and subconscious minds together in harmony. For when you impress your subconscious mind with what you consciously desire, your subconscious will do what ever is necessary for its attainment. It will bring your desire to you, bring you to it, or guide you, and/or bring you to the people, to the books, to the movies, or even guide you through your dreams. These are also some of the ways in which your subconscious communicates with you as well. We call them coincidences and disregard the rest as silly notions or superstitions. Any way it can, your subconscious will help you to attain your desire. Become aware of who you really are.

The subconscious has resources beyond our conscious awareness to get things accomplished for us. As you are constantly thinking, in sub-vocalization or aloud, your subconscious is always listening and always responding. It is always there with you, because it is you. It is the all-powerful you, the "You" in the image of God, "You." Things happen in your life because of you. There are no coincidences only events that coincide.

Sooner or later you have to trust in something, you might as well start with trusting your Self. The unlimited abilities of the subconscious you are beyond comprehension. "Mysterious are the ways of the Lord." "Endless are the ways of the Lord." "Ask, believing, and you shall receive!"

As you begin to understand and know yourself better, as you start to understand who you really are; you will learn to practice using the power you have to create a better and more peaceful life for yourself.

Furthermore, you can only recognize in another person what you know of in yourself. Learn about your true Self. If you were to look at me and develop an opinion, good or bad, you would not see in me more than you know about yourself. This is not only true about first impressions, which are pretty strong in themselves, but even after a time has gone by and you have come to know a little more about me. The most you can recognize in me is what you can see in yourself.

As we grow, interact, and influence one another, we add to each other's character, which allows us to recognize these characteristics in others. Then also, when you have learned to love yourself, you can learn to love another, and with that, you are then also returning love to God.

Faith

"If you have the Faith of a mustard seed..."

Faith and belief are like a brother and sister that depend on each other, that confide in one another, and that are in harmony with each other.

Faith is expectation. It is almost like taking things for granted, like the belief that your desired outcome has to be fulfilled. Faith is not blind. It needs the energy of your belief in what you desire that it will happen, to make it happen. Faith, in a manner of speaking, is like you are certain; you just know that what you desire will be. Here are a couple of examples of the kind of thinking or sub-vocalization you may find. You might say to yourself; "I just knew..." "It was like I was hit with a ton of bricks." That is how obviously sure you are about something, and that is "faith."

Again, this is the process. You have a thought. You create a desire. Thought is followed by energy to bring about your desire. If there is no conviction, or if you create a negative thought in there somewhere, you negate (cancel), or change the original thought with that quiet negating thought.

To demonstrate a desire, that is to purposely manifest an outcome into physical reality from a thought, you must have faith at the conscious level. In turn, this will impress your subconscious to bring it about and *"...in accordance to your faith"* it will.

Try this experiment to see if you can become aware of your thinking that follows this thought. Sit quietly and create a desire. Repeat the following statement: "I desire a million dollars to be manifested in perfect ways right in my lap right now." What did you think of immediately after you made this request? Write it down and look at how you were thinking.

If you got the million dollars, congratulation, let me know. You do not need this book. If like everyone I have tried this experiment with, your last thought was, "yeah sure!" or some semblance of disbelief, well you got what you thought. Nothing! Of all the people I have tried this experiment with, the first thought that comes to their mind is, "it's impossible." Therefore, by the nature of the thought that followed your claim, as it were, would not even have a chance to begin to manifest physically.

Note: Because money was on there mind, I have had people come back to me saying they unexpectedly came into some money later that day or shortly thereafter.

Your reasoning and logic can get in your way, or you can use them to help you to demonstrate your desires. You can use reason and logic to assure yourself that you deserve to receive what you desire. You can mentally create an argument in your favor as to why you should have what you have asked to be manifested into your life. When you ask for a desire to be fulfilled, you must believe that the Universe, your Higher Power, Infinite Intelligence, or God will provide the way. Do not negate the thought with an after thought that says, "Its impossible!" or "I'm not worthy of it." Argue your way through it. Convince your Self that you are worthy, because you are!

By the way, if there are no coincidences, then how does one win the lottery? For that matter, why are there so many losers, so to speak? And in some lottery drawings, why are there multiple winners?

One more thing, faith is a very powerful force. "Faith can move mountains," but to where would you move them? You have to take responsibility for your thoughts, just as you take responsibility for your behavior. To where would you move the mountains? You would be the cause and what effect would be the outcome? Would you move the mountains into the ocean and single-handedly create a tidal wave on the other side of the world that might devastate entire communities?

Responsibility

Your subconscious is objective, impersonal in nature. It does not second-guess you. It just delivers what you ask for, and also by your habit thinking. It is "The You" that you are. You are its reflection and its creation. Through a whole complex network of communication and modalities beyond comprehension, your subconscious brings about your desire, truly in mysterious ways. You are it, and it is you.

You have the conscious power and ability to create by your thinking. Understand this and take responsibility for your life. You can blame others for your lack, but at some point you would do well to recognize your position and responsibility. Take responsibility for attracting all of the good in your life, as well as the trials, misfortunes and hard knocks. Remember too, there is wonderful knowledge to be found in adversity. You just have to be open to see it, acknowledge it, and move forward.

Humans have a (response) (ability) that animals do not have. A wounded animal for example, will attack the nearest moving thing, regardless of what caused its wound. We humans have the ability to think and then respond. Do not any longer just react to situations, especially those that may offend you. Take time to respond to situations with thoughtfulness.

Think of "reaction" as a response without pausing to think. Reacting to, is also a link in the cycle of cause and effect. Action causes reaction, which cause another reaction, and so on and so forth.

Response-ability in this case means, taking control of your thoughts before you act or re-act. If you practice in peace and with patience, the next time you are in a stressful situation you will be better able, better prepared to think of how you are going to respond.

For example: To become prepared for a fight, a good boxer practices fighting in peace and with patience long before entering into the ring for a match. In the physical realm, this is how a boxer prepares for a match or a title fight. In the mental realm, this physical practice allows the boxer to develop confidence. Being in the match is not the time to lose control, and it is not the time to practice fighting techniques either. The practice is done when there is no fight. So take control of your "Response Ability."

How do you deal with anger? Use your Response Ability.

Ask yourself first, "How should I respond in this situation?" As a general example: "I've just been insulted about my ability to function and I'm angry." Pause and think; "Why am I angry? What am I afraid of? How should I respond in this situation?" This is very hard to do when you are in the thick of things. If you practice in peace and with patience, you will be less easily moved to an emotion that will cause you more difficulty in whatever relationship you are dealing. You will be less likely to shoot from the hip, so to speak. You can make intelligent decisions on how you will respond and what your response will be.

"I accept responsibility for my actions, now what will I do to bring about a more satisfying life for myself?" Always ask for guidance; ask for right-action in your life. Say to your self, "Let me act to attain my highest good." Create a wonderful life for yourself. Have faith and expect to have wonderful changes come about in your life as you purposefully change your thinking.

Forces of Good and Evil, by Jennifer Canosa

Just a Thought

If the Christ is a level of consciousness then...

People have discussed the subject of the anti-Christ for as long as I can remember, as I was growing-up in Chicago. For me as a child, hearing people talk on the subject of the anti-Christ was at times pretty frightening. I could only imagine some wicked, almost all-powerful demon taking over the world and reeking havoc on all of creation.

Some people, of standing, have even pointed to others by name and inferred that they are or might be the anti-Christ. Some people, with credibility in their communities, have made the suggestion of where the anti-Christ will be born in the near future, pointing to another country and sometimes producing strong arguments to support their claims. Some of these people even get on T.V. to make their proclamations. Now that is really scary!

"The Christ is within you." "Pray to the Christ within you."

"Cast your burden on the Christ within you." (Is this a hint of the truth?)

I submit this argument to you for your consideration.

If Buddha and Jesus attained a level of awareness that transcended them beyond the conscious mind awareness, and the level itself that they attained is the Christ consciousness level; then the ego, driving the immature conscious mind and the undisciplined personality, the ego full of fear and doubt, is the anti-Christ.

The ego in this state, is the opposite (opposing) and limiting level of consciousness.

Many years ago psychologists had divided the human condition into three aspects of consciousness. They are the ego, the id, and the super-ego. This was a fairly well accepted theory and some psychologists today hold the theory to be a true working model. How they treat for disorders in their patients varies from practitioner to practitioner.

The ego's main purpose seems to be the driving force in life, which is, staying alive. It was considered to be the factor that has helped us to stay alive as a species as well. The ego's basis for survival is its belief about itself, and what is safe and what is not, in other words, its primary driving force is fear.

The ego's self-esteem drives us to success or failure, and if you let it, it will run your life. The ego centered, the personality expressed, the "I must have this, this is mine, mine, mine…" is the brat as it were. Or the, "I can't do that, I can't do this, I'm afraid." In addition, the ego says things like, "You can do anything you want to do! Take it, who is going to know?" Statements of this nature are of course based on fear of lack. The ego the is… *The devil?*

Perhaps you have notice something like this happening to you: You are sitting quietly contemplating or affirming, and you have this negating thought that just creeps into your consciousness. You find yourself following this thought, meaning, it got your attention. You realize that it is negative in nature and immediately dismiss it, which disarms that negative though.

I would like you to give this concept a moment of reflection. You are sitting in peace, attending a thought for good and suddenly a fear, worry or concern, just pops up seemingly out of nowhere. How can this be? Why would you have a fear sponsored thought at a time like this? How can you have two thoughts going on at the same time? Some say you cannot. Well, either you can, or the scared and negating ego aspect of you projects thoughts so fast that you do not always realize them. This is also true. But you say to yourself, "Hey I'm doing my affirmations for my higher good, how can I be considering a whole scenario of concern about a loved one, or some terrible thing coming to pass?"

Here is another example, one that may be easier with which to relate. You are driving your car and a great deal of the time your thoughts are elsewhere, daydreaming or just thinking of other things besides driving. Sometimes you are aware of thinking of things other than driving safely to your destination and sometimes you are not. This happens at 15 mph or at 60 mph regardless of any aspect of danger.

As in daydreaming, in this way too, while affirming for your higher good, you can send out a negating thought along with your honest desires without realizing you have done so. Let us label this that part of your personality, your ego, "defending itself" from losing control of you to your higher consciousness.

An affirmation of your truth need only be made once, with faith, for your subconscious mind to bring it about for you. In my case, I believed this to be true. Nevertheless, only when I studied and practiced asking, did I realize why some of the things I would ask for came about immediately, some took time and some things did not show up in my life at all. An after thought, or negative something of my habit thinking, would change the outcome of what I had asked or claimed that I wanted. But, I only realized this after a good deal of practice reflecting and paying attention to my thoughts as I made my declarations or affirmation of what things I wanted to manifest or achieve. It was that aspect of me, this ego thing that seems to be its own individual self. It would pipe in, and with the same energy that follows any thought, as it is universal law, and negate my conscious desire. That sub-vocal negative thought is still my thought, my ego. It is not another individual, it is still my thought. And so, it is my thinking that causes my failure to attain that which I desire.

Fear and doubt are, in my opinion, life's most hindering and greatest destructive forces. So debilitating is fear that it can lock your body up to immobility and get you killed.

Doubt is uncertainty and lack of confidence. It is one of fear's children. It will keep you from moving forward and progressing in life. Moreover, "I can't" is one of the most limiting of words or phrases in the Standard American English Language.

Give this scenario a little of your attention. You are in a burning building with no way to escape except to jump out through the window near where you are standing. You are three flights up, on the third floor, you are afraid of heights and you are afraid to jump. On the one hand, you know you have a chance to survive, if you could only get yourself to jump out through the open window so close to where you are standing. You look out the window to the grass below, but you stop to think; "I can't jump, I could be seriously injured. I'll land on my face or I'll land on my head, and I could get killed." This internal dialog is what causes you to freeze with fear, while a raging fire is right behind you and it will consume you without question.

That is your ego full of fear and doubt keeping you from moving forward. As well, when wonderful opportunities come your way, it is your ego reminding you that you are just not worthy of such good fortune. This ego, this devil, keeps you from progressing and moving forward.

Your ego, self-esteem, your higher consciousness, and your thoughts are all you. None of them have to be your enemy. You can gently bring these aspects of "you" into harmony. You can control your thinking and start removing the garbage that you have learned to sense by paying attention to your sub-vocalization.

Clear your conscious mind of negativity. Do it, in time, by filling your mind with wonderful and positive thoughts and affirmations daily. Emulate the lives of the many wonderful and successful people on Earth. They are in your communities. Look for them. Talk to successful people; learn about them and how they came to be successful. Do what they have done. In the meantime make the time to study and learn about who you really are.

The id, your conscious-self, mostly acting through the ego, mainly reckons with the thoughts you have in the constant now. You think and you know that you are, therefore, it becomes difficult to recognize the other aspects of you. It is the "you" that acts out your daily life. You think, you read, you work, and all of that. And by choice, the id you, can take control of your life for your higher good. Ask, affirm, or pray for guidance and for help to understand, and then pay attention. Look for the answers to your questions.

The super-ego has been described as a higher state of consciousness than is the id or the ego. It is the state you achieve when you actively take control of your habit thinking away from your ego. When you take control of your thinking, then you start to remove some of the struggle in your life. Moreover, we say you have developed self-discipline.

With regard to your ego, you can start to challenge some of your fears. Some say, you take control of your neurosis in order to manage your daily affairs more effectively. But that is a good start.

I believe that the super-ego is the subconscious mind, that which is or rather which leads us to the Soul and to the Christ-Consciousness. The real Anti-Christ is the negative belief system that so many have developed over time. One very common belief that must be over come is the thought of not being worthy of God's love and all the treasures he has to offer you.

Become the Cause of Your Life

When I graduated from college, not so long ago, I studied hard, and all that. I do not believe that I had the attitude that society owed me a job. I just expected to be hired immediately after graduation. I knew I could become an excellent elementary school teacher. All of my evaluations seemed to indicate that and supported my thinking. Many of the teachers that I worked with in elementary schools during my studies made kind comments to me about how good I was with the kids.

So, why did it take me so long to get my career off the ground? And, it did.

I learned early on to do things that would enhance my resume. As I went through college, I put a great deal of thought into writing my resume. After graduation from the university, I immediately began to send out over 100 resumes, and I got one very poor interview for a teaching position.

I was given jobs and job offers that were less than satisfying. Some of these job offers were not even for teaching positions. I could not get the teaching jobs that I thought I wanted.

In asking people I knew and past professors for their opinions on my resume, everyone that I spoke with said my resume was impressive. Everyone seemed to like me. So, "what was going on?"

I felt dejected and hopeless at first. I had given up a really good foundation that I had built in real estate sales, "for this!" I had little fleeting thoughts of regret about having left my career as a realtor. Like, "Three and a half years of work in real estate out the window." "What would all of that effort in real estate have brought me now if I hadn't quit?" Had I started to develop resentment towards my new chosen field? Yes, but I had not recognized it as resentment as yet. Fleeting thoughts as they were, I still had them and they were still my thoughts.

I received support for my feelings of self-pity. Here are some of the answers that came to me from inside of me, and from conversations with past instructors and peers. (By the way, many of my peers found jobs almost immediately, in what seemed to be a very difficult job market.)

"She knew someone in the system." "You just have to hang in there and pay your dues." "They don't really want to hire a man, because of the risk of law suits working with kids." "Most principals are women and they are going to hire young women fresh into their careers. They're more easily manageable." "You're just too old. Their insurance won't let them hire you." "You should get an attorney and sue their asses for discrimination."

Since I had left my career as a realtor to go to the university to become a teacher, I started working as a substitute teacher to earn my keep. After graduation, I kept on as a substitute teacher in hopes I would someday get hired on as a full-time teacher, and to pay my bills. I knew there was a way to enjoy using the knowledge I had attained from all of that effort and study. I loved teaching, and all this work could not have been for nothing.

I planned, I worked, I sent out more resumes, and I tried to be very accommodating. Still, I received not one interview with an elementary school.

Nothing satisfying came to me in the way of emotional or monetary gain. I found myself with more time on my hands. I resolved to bide my time and try to enjoy what I had. "Now there's a positive note."

I began reading a little for enjoyment. None of what I read were text-book material. I read things that I had been interested in reading not so very long ago. Then, I started reading a little more. Interestingly, one book would lead me to another. Without realizing it at first, slowly, over time, I found myself starting back on the path to a philosophy I had for-gotten. I found myself studying a philosophy that gave me peace many years ago. I read, and I pondered and reflected, and I grew in awareness. I grew in awareness of my thinking and in the world around me.

One day I saw an ad in the paper for a part-time teaching position at a private college. I sent my resume, with interest, not thinking much of it, when within a few days I was called for an interview with this college. **Understand that this resume went out with no concerns or excitement, no doubts or any other negating thoughts, only an interest in the opportunity.**

After they had called me to set-up an appointment, I noticed all sorts of things were going through my mind at that time. These thoughts I was having at that time were less than positive.

To shorten the story, I got the job with the college and lost it, even before I began to work. I blamed luck and circumstance. But this time I had no resentment toward them, nor with Susan, the woman with whom I had interviewed.

She was warm and kind and supportive. She even suggested that maybe the next term would be a more convenient time to start me, and that she would keep my resume.

Basically, I believed that the circumstances being as they were, could not allow for the starting date that the college needed. I took her comment about calling me in the future as a polite gesture on her part, not thinking anything more than that.

I continued to study the books that I was being "attracted to." I took a closer look at my attitude and why things were happening to me the way they did.

From what I had been studying, I thought to myself, "Could I have really been the cause of my lack and my inability to get my career started?"

And with those questions in mind, my thinking started to become a little clearer. I practiced becoming more aware of my thoughts and how I felt about things. I started to notice the many negative thoughts I was still carrying. First, I started to let go of self-pity. Moreover, I began to let go of thoughts of fear, lack, and doubt.

A few months later the same wonderful Susan called me back with a job offer that lead me to a very satisfying part-time teaching position at that college. **Coincidence?** I do not, in my heart, believe so.

This job still gave me time to read and study success and what success really means. And study I did. As I changed my old and useless thinking habits, my life changed more rapidly in my favor.

Was my resume really all that important? Trust me! Writing a resume, like goal setting, is of great value. It helps you in many ways; it also helps to create clarity in your thinking. However, without belief, faith, and positive action, you can write wonderful resumes until you are 100 years old. What would be the end result? Well, what do you think? By the way, a second and third very satisfying teaching opportunity came to me, and my resumes were looked at as an after thought.

Since that time, and with much study and practice, my life is falling into place very nicely thank you. I say IS, because life is, and success is, an on going process, and *IS* always changing.

Consciously take control of your life by asking your Higher Self, Infinite Intelligence, or what ever you prefer to call it, for the things you want to attain in your life. Begin to change your life on purpose with purpose. Ask for guidance. Declare your desires. Practice asking, and expect to receive what you have asked to come into your life.

Let me take a minute to explain the "willingness to receive" aspect. For example, looking at how communication and how a contract work together. A contract communicates an idea. Of course, in this case what we are looking at is the aspect of communication with your "Self."

In a contract, the fundamental requirement between two or more people is that one person must be ready, willing and able to give, or do something, and the other person must be ready, willing and able to accept; to receive. At this point, we then have an agreement. Still, the contract is not complete until it is executed, until both parties have fulfilled their part of the agreement.

The subconscious is always listening and ready, willing and able to bring you what you have asked to come into your reality. For your part, the only things you must consciously do are to accept and receive. It is very much like the execution aspect of a contract. The difference is that you will receive, and what you receive is given to you dependent upon your faith. It is dependent on your ability to accept all that you have asked for, and the clarity with which you have asked.

How do you desire to have your life change?

Remember this: You are the driving force in and of your life! "What you think about, you bring about."

I Can Take It

I sort through King-sized obstacles,
Desiring triumph for a new dawn.

I see I chose these games of life,
That bring feelings of a Pawn.

Yet I'll grasp and wield inspiring thoughts,
While planning out my dreams.

For times I've truly lived I've learned,
A Pawn can take a King.

Written by
Vito DeLiso

SECTION TWO

Goal Setting

Goal setting is an important process, but it does not work as well and as easily, without the knowledge of that wondrous ancient wisdom passed down to us by our ancestors.

"Ask and you shall receive." "Seek and ye shall find."

"Knock and the door shall be opened unto you." "Take action."

Goal Setting/Major purpose

The seven steps to goal setting is a helpful method for clarifying your desires. When setting goals, or if you want to impress your subconscious so that you may obtain your desires, your goals should be written and written clearly so there is no doubt as to what you want to accomplish.

I have added to this book an academic method, or call it a "formal method" of goal setting. I have used this seven steps method to teach goal setting in the past in academic settings and in seminars. Because this method works, I have included it in this book.

It is my belief that this method works only because of the facts presented in the previous portions of this book. Will these seven steps work if you have had no previous knowledge (awareness) of the aforesaid description of the nature of reality? Of course, because these seven steps still follow the law of what you attract in desire, purpose, intention, belief, faith, action, and results.

Note: Always start your goal setting with what you intend to accomplish. Develop for yourself a clear understanding of the end result of what you desire to achieve. Set your goals with the end in mind.

As Napoleon Hill said, "Anybody can wish for riches, and most people do, but only few know that a definite plan, plus a burning desire for wealth, are the only dependable means of accumulating wealth."

Clear thinking

Reduce your desire/goal, end result, to two or three clearly written sentences. **In writing!** Carry it with you on a card and affirm it daily. Do not cause yourself to worry. Ships come in easily over clear and calm waters. There is no need to worry, only affirm and follow through. Just do it! Get busy now. Create purpose in your life now and always.

Accomplish one thing and find new endeavors. Keep creating, that is why you are here. Create and be amazed always.

Note: Understand that we all make personal and business decisions based on our personal beliefs, attitudes, experiences, environment, and educational background.

The basis for all functions of goal setting is planning and organizing. The difference between a goal and a wish is the action taken to produce the end result, along with the belief and faith that you will reach your goal. And so it goes with wishing a problem would go away, versus finding a solution to the problem.

The Seven Steps in Goal Setting, Problem Solving and Decision Making

1. Clearly define your goal or problem. IN WRITING!
  * Exactness is the key to the first step.
  * Create a statement that clearly says what you intend to accomplish.
  * If it is a problem that you wish to solve, clearly define the problem.

2. Gather information
  * Similar goals/problems were achieved or solved by others somewhere, at sometime. Look at what others have done. Do what others have done. Use the scientific method. There is a solution to every problem. I personally believe in the statement that "The solution precedes the problem."

3. Interpret information
  * Based on the information you have gathered and assessed, you must first decide if your goal is feasible and worthwhile. If not "don't spin your wheels," move on to other things!

4. Developing solutions
* Study and examine your options. Determine from where you are now in life, from your point of view, various possible and probable outcomes based on your findings.

5. Select the best practical solution
* Create a plan of action, or follow an existing plan.
* Set a time to start and implement your plan of action.
* Plant the seed and take care of it. Do not condemn it. Have faith and take time for assessment of the plan of action to help you to stay on track.
* Set a definite completion time. Be realistic. Seeds need time to grow into giant trees. They do not become a redwood forest overnight. Be flexible.

6. Put your solution into effect. "Plan your Work—then Work your Plan"
* Planning is the foundation of what ever you desire to build. It is the beginning of action. The thought comes first and it carries great amounts of energy. Work your plan. Keep up the action of caring for your seed (your desired outcome).
* Do your part, which you must. "God helps those who help themselves."

7. Evaluate the effectiveness of your plan of action as time passes
Have patience and be flexible. *"As conditions change all things change."*
* Time should be made periodically along the way to accomplishing a goal for assessments and evaluation of your plan of action. This will help to insure the effectiveness of your plan of action as things change. It will also help you to make certain that your goal can be reached with the chosen plan, or to take the opportunity to make modifications to the plan.

I would like to leave you with these words that hit home for me from a lecture given by Anthony J. Fisichella. **Idea, Ideal, Idol.**

When you have reached your goal remember these three words: Idea, ideal, idol.

First you have the **idea**, a goal in mind, and your purpose.

Ideal; you bring your goal to fruition, and you get to enjoy it.

Idol, to idolize, it is a wonder to behold. Caution: When we say, "Your car is at idle," we mean the motor is running but the car is not going anywhere. As wonderful as your accomplishment may be, do not become stagnant. Do not fall into a trap of becoming idle/idol. Remember; "move on." To idolize can cause your end.

Remember too: To become old does not mean to become idle/idol, although some would make that suggestion. Many great people reached the pinnacle of their fields of interest between the ages of fifty and seventy years of age.

SECTION THREE

The Circle of Influence

Why We Would Create a Circle of Influence

"When two or more come together in my name..."

And so it is that when your subconscious mind and your conscious mind come together over an idea, it is done.

Remember your subconscious mind is always listening and ready to give you what you desire. It does not relate to good or bad! I think it was John-Roger who said it best in his book, *Spiritual Warrior:* Remember = Re member, to become a member again with your real self.

When you purposefully ask for something, your subconscious is already in harmony with your desire. It is ready to bring it about; unless you change your conscious mind, or have not yet changed your negative thinking habit. Stay positive with your thought and your desire. Bring yourself, your conscious mind, in harmony with your subconscious mind and it will be done. Two minds coming together over the same idea, "When two or more come together in my name..."

Coming together; are in agreement; are in harmony with one another; the power of thought is greatly intensified when two or more "people" come together. This brings us back to belief. Then the rule would be; belief in the idea and belief in one another to commit to the idea to bring it about into this reality. "Every man is a golden link in the chain of my success" (Shinn).

"Two or more people coming together..." This is what Napoleon Hill called, creating a "Master Mind." The idea is, bringing together a group of people that you can depend on, into your confidence. Bringing people together with skills and talents that you do not necessarily possess and that are committed to seeing your idea to fruition, because they believe in it as well. This is the basic function of a board of directors in a corporation. In addition, this is why you hire others to work with you in any endeavor. It is the commonality of a goal, along with self-interest and self-satisfaction. It is their belief in your goal, along with their own motivations such as love, wealth and self-expression that will bring about the wanted end results.

I believe no one does anything totally on his or her own, except die. And understandably, most of us do not even want to do that alone. Do you think you were meant to be alone? Do you think there might be a reason you are on a planet with six billion other people?

Developing a circle of influence

Make a list of the names of the all of the people you know. At some point in time you may call on them for friendship, for fun, for a business endeavor, or for whatever reason. If you have not done this in the past, do so now and just keep it.

First you have to trust that you will have help in the accomplishment of your desire. Your subconscious will attract to you those individuals who will best serve your purpose, if you ask. So, you do not have to pressure your closest friends into helping you with your idea. Have faith. Trust that it will be done and that the above collection of names may come in handy.

Take care not to judge who can, who is more able, or who will help you. You never know **who** on your list is most likely to come through for you, or who is best suited for the job. It could easily be the least likely person you know who could become most beneficial to you in your endeavor.

Where do you start? Maybe you do not know many people, because you do not get out much, or you are new to the area. Get out and meet people. Get involved with people. Today's catchword is "Network." This is not a new concept either. Join clubs that are truly of interest to you. Take classes of interest to you and attend social events you might enjoy. They have people there with similar interests as yours, or they would not be there. Go to places where you can feel comfortable and get to know the people there. Find out what else they are interested in, what else you might have in common.

When you find someone you feel you can trust, someone like yourself, share your idea with him or her. See if they show any interest in working with you on your project. If you find you are wrong about someone, do not condemn or make an issue of it, move on to someone else.

Trust and be judicious. Remember, judgmental is labeling good or bad, able or not able. Judicious is making wise and positively thoughtful decisions. You do not need to spill your guts about your project and then worry, "Did I give away too much?" "Did I give away too much information about my idea?" Ask your Higher Self for guidance. Learn to sense your feelings about people and situations. As Dan Millman wrote in his book *Way of the Peaceful Warrior*, "Lose your mind and come to your senses." Learn to feel.

Let us talk about networking, creating a circle of influence.

First of all I do not believe you can motivate anyone anymore than you can give someone a headache. It is not yours to give. Likewise, motivation comes from within one's-self; it too is not yours to give. But excitement is infectious. Enthusiasm will get my attention. Goals can be shared ideas.

Furthermore, if you can show me the possibility that I might have a better life, self-satisfaction, a lifestyle of luxury, of wealth and abundance; if I like what I see of your life, of you, then likewise, I might develop a desire to help you to obtain your goal. Tell me that with your help or guidance, and with your wonderful idea, I can achieve success too. With that I may well be influenced to join you in your endeavor.

These are some basic reasons for you to understand and become good at networking.

EMPOWERMENT CAREER ENHANCEMENT PROMOTING YOURSELF

Empowerment

Example: Before we talk about empowerment, does anyone like attorneys?

Suddenly you find yourself saying, "I need an attorney because of a $70,000.00 law suit filed against me. Does anybody know a good attorney?"

Do you think that in helping me to secure the service of a good and caring attorney? This in itself might cause me to remember you when I meet someone who is looking for a service or product that you provide. Would that not make you look like the kind of a person who is knowledgeable, resourceful, involved, and interested in others; interested in me? Did you just empower me to possibly help someone else, and that I might return the favor at some point in our business relationship? Can we agree that the more people you develop a relationship with the more empowered you become? Does not that relationship that you have developed also empower someone else and create more potential business for yourself?

Career Enhancement; Promoting Yourself

I suggest that you develop a one-sentence statement about yourself, like a one sentence advertisement. When you have or create the opportunity to meet someone new, they will know something about you or the business you do, right then and there. For example, at most of the meetings I have attended away from our organization, everyone in attendance, in turn, introduces themselves and the name of the company that they represent.

In years past, as a spokes person and coordinator for a nonprofit organization I worked with, I was always on the lookout for volunteer mentors. When I would meet someone new I would introduce myself with a statement like, "Hi my name is Tony DeLiso, and I'm the Volunteer Director for Cities in Schools of Broward County, Dropout Prevention Program." Or when someone asked me, "What do you do?" I was prepared with this short but descriptive answer.

So too, if you are looking for a job, create a one sentence concise work related statement about what you do or would like to do.

This statistic I am about to relate is an older one, but I am sure you will find it to be pretty much correct for today as well. Newspapers, state job services and many of the private employment services combined, represent only about 20% of the total job market.

What do you do to penetrate that less advertised and greater job market, the one where most of the "above average paying" jobs exists? Certainly, you can go to school and prepare yourself for your field of interest. Many companies recruit at college and vocational school campuses. You can immediately begin by letting people know who you are. Make friends. Network and market yourself. Sell yourself to others, for business and for friendships. Let us not forget that networking is mostly just socializing and meeting people.

Where else in the world can you go to meet people? Someone I heard of in sales once said, "Go downtown, throw a rock up in the air and go stand where it falls. Start there! Talk to the first person that walks by." You have got to get involved to get people to know who you are and what you can do for them.

I know a very bright young woman who graduated with a 3.7 grade point average. After she received her bachelor degree, then of course she wanted to begin developing her career. We talked about writing a resume. I suggested she write a cover letter along with a body of her experiences, and that she might include her references at the end of the resume instead of saying, "references upon request." She said, "I don't know anyone I can use as a reference besides you." I have known her and her family for a while, and so I said that of course she could use my name. Then I asked her, of all of those professors and academic advisors that she knew from the university, who could she call upon for a letter of recommendation? She said, "I never knew any of my teachers' names and I only saw an academic advisor at the university once." And with her wonderful academic record, she never involved herself at school. She never made the effort to get to know any of her professors so that she might go back to them at some point in time and ask for a letter of recommendation.

We need each other. We need to know other people. Make friends; develop working and lasting relationships.

Networking and Community Service

Get involved in community service. What a great way to meet people, grow professionally and grow on a personal level as well. As a volunteer, I logged over 100 hours working in the elementary schools and a high school in my community. That was a very satisfying experience for me. It was in doing that volunteer work that I decided to become a teacher. I had only intended to commit to 35 hours when I had first decided to become involved in community service through the college I was attending at the time. Can you imagine the kind of growth I realized from those experiences of working and teaching?

I am talking about networking and making new acquaintances; not to mention the gains in my personal growth. What am I talking about when I say networking is empowerment? All of us will have to sell ourselves at some point if we want a job, or to become accepted by any organization or for any reason. What I am talking about is getting involved in your community. There are many worthwhile organizations in your community and around the world. Try one!

SECTION FOUR

Foundation Complete

Your foundation is ready on which to build. Now what will you build upon it?

Affirming Your Truth

"If thou canst believe, all things are possible to him that believeth."
(Mark 9:23)

Affirm your desires and know that you will receive them into your reality.

This is what a New Years resolution is about, is it not? New Year, new you, and starting the year fresh. "Out with the old in with the new." Out with old thoughts that have not worked for you; in with new and positive…Desires…We resolve. We sometimes write out resolutions and even become inspired by doing so. And then nothing happens. Why? Nothing happens, because we did not hold the thought. It might be, because we really did not believe in the possibility of attaining our desires and accomplishing our goals. We negated our resolutions, our desires, with old negative thinking.

Old thinking, or a trigger, is the cause of many of the problems in our lives. You must start to work on clearing out all those old negative triggering thoughts. Decide to begin now to clear out all of those old triggering thoughts that started collecting in your mind, since God knows when. Those old triggers that cause fear, doubt, sadness, anger, resentment, and et cetera. Triggers are reminders of past situations. We react emotionally and often automatically in a new situation, because the new situation we are living reminds us to react in this manner or that automatically, and most often we do not even know why.

Here is a textbook example of a trigger due to an old experience. As a young girl she was afraid of Santa Claus. Her parents could not understand her fear, and they dismissed it. As a young woman she had a disdain for men with beards, especially if their beard was white. The alleged cause of the triggering mechanism to men with beards found during hypnotherapy; when she was just a toddler she was given a white rabbit as a gift. For whatever reason, and maybe in the manner in which the rabbit was presented to her, the white rabbit startled her and that trauma was never resolved. Therefore, her unresolved fear which began with the white rabbit from her childhood experience, had been carried forward with her into her young adult period and became the trigger of her strong discomfort with bearded men. In this case recognizing the origin of the problem was enough to deal with, and of course, overcome the unwarranted negative affects of her dislike toward men with beards.

The cause of some of your triggers may or may not ever be recognized by you. If your reactions to a situation are not favorable, then ask yourself, "Why am I reacting as I am?" And once again, "What am I afraid of?" If you never find the cause, can you overcome an adverse reaction to a situation? You can decide to affirm to treat everyone and all situations with understanding and from a more positive standpoint. So the answer would be, yes you can overcome an adverse reaction to a situation, by your willingness to judiciously find a peaceful resolve.

Triggers are generally considered negative. Those are the ones to which we pay most attention. For example, "He makes me so angry. He knows how to push all of my buttons." They are old and hindering thoughts (buttons that someone may "push"). They are not even true anymore, because they are old; from previous times. Do not let yourself relive them. Respond judiciously with kindness, understanding and with love.

Then, there are those untrue old programs and phrases that hinder our progress today. Words from our past that over time we have come to believe are true about ourselves, such as: "You're a spoil brat." "Oh, do you have to be so clumsy?" "Go to your room, you're giving me a headache." "Look at these grades; you'll be digging ditches for the rest of your life." "I was never any good at math."

Unfortunately, there are those really hurtful phrases that come from our caretakers and even from people we may love and put our trust in, such as: "Get away from me." "If I didn't have these kids I'd…" "You're the reason I can't…" And what about, "I don't love you anymore."

Of course, there are even more and profoundly worse things said and done to children and by children every day. Some of us hear these phrases and comments for much of our lives. We do collect a lot of garbage. Our minds, our egos, can become filled with old untrue programming triggers. When the ego is in control the conscious you tends to believe, deal with and from, the perspective of this garbage thinking that it has collected, and therefore, we identify with it. When we make this identity, over time, we start to consider ourselves different from the next person. Thus, we see ourselves as an individual. "Now I standout." "Now I know who I am." "I am an Individual." "This may be my lot in life, I'm yucky." "I'm weird." "I'm strange, but I am defined." Your subconscious knows better, its part of The All That Is.

Then ego says, "I'm an individual but I want to belong." We will join all sorts of groups and manner of groups of people that we find we can relate to and befriend. "I can't wait 'til I can leave home." "Me too! Hey let's hang out together." "My parents are…" "My teachers are…" "The other kids at school are…" Gangs, streets, bars, and so on are, well, as the old saying goes, places where "Birds of a feather flock together." The commonality of these groups may be the "negative thinking" each has, but this also makes for binding relationships; perhaps not healthy ones, but binding just the same.

Even if we are raised in better environments; even if it is a loving environment, we identify and are individualized as we see our selves to be. Nevertheless, we want to belong and be acknowledged as well. Here are some examples of sub-vocalization of "identity" wanting to be a part of someone or something: "If I take this class, I'll…" "If I join this country club, it will…" "If I join that social group, I'll…" We want to be individuals, but at the same time, we want to belong.

When we do join, do we get to be happy? How many of us just express ourselves in what we really love to do? Your subconscious knows better, it is part of The All That Is. Just ask it.

Can you really get rid of the thousands of old negative thoughts that you have collected over the years? Maybe you can and maybe you cannot. However, you will not at all, if you do not start by showing yourself love. If you do not take care of yourself as though you are your own "best parent" in the world, then of course you will continue longing. If you do not start "taking in" healthy thoughts about yourself and identifying with those kinds of thoughts that are for your highest good, if you do not begin with what you now know and are seeking to learn, then how can you move forward?

So, "Out with the Old and in with the New."
New and wonderful thoughts about you and what your life and your identity are to become.

It is your life and your choice as to how you want to live it. Remember to pay attention to your sub-vocalization. Pay attention to what you are thinking about as much and as often as you can. Your thoughts carry just as much power as any intentional affirmation.

Affirmations impress the subconscious mind by constant reiteration; holding your truth in your conscious mind. Your desire is your truth. Affirmations of positive thoughts create positive results in your life; they must, because your subconscious is always listening. Remember, the same is true for the opposite.

You will become aware, in time and with practice, you do make affirmations daily and moment-by-moment. Your subconscious, as I have stated time and again, is always listening to you. It is always ready to respond to your thoughts (your sub-vocalization) and words. Affirmations are your thoughts, prayers, and gentle demands, on purpose with purpose. Proclaim what you will.

I am writing this, as I said, to confirm the reality of the attainment of desires/goals by changing your mind. Pay attention to what you think about and by talking to yourself with loving care. Again, it is important to recognize that your gentle claims, your goals and desires, your demands and your prayers, are all your thoughts, and that is what affirmations are.

"Awe, affirmations don't work. I've tried them." They will not work, if YOU do not THINK they WILL! If that is your thinking, then that is what you get. Your subconscious knows better, it is part of The All That Is. That is your identity.

"On Earth as it is in Heaven." Earth is your reality. Heaven is your mind. You bring these two together to create; or more correctly, to co-create.

Repeating the affirmations in this section will work. Make them your own. Read them over and over until they become your own. Create a belief that they are true statements and they will become true for you. Alter them as you wish. Create your own affirmations from your imagination. With practice you can develop a wonderful imagination and proceed to create. This is the real magic. **This is your power within!**

Ownership of an affirmation is the key! *"Man can only be what he sees himself to be"* (Shinn).

In other words, relating a statement you make to or about yourself is ownership. All statements you make that follow the words; I, I am, mine, and et cetera show ownership. They tell your subconscious mind, "put this in memory to act upon it," and your subconscious does. If this sounds simplistic, it may because I am trying to be for our purposes here. Yet, that is what really happens anyway.

Again, "What you think about, you bring about." Your subconscious just gives you what you ask for; positive or negative, good or bad.

Start affirming your truth

As you begin to affirm your truth, take the time to calm your body and your mind; remember "…*calm waters.*"

Dr. Joseph Murphy suggests bringing your affirmation to bed with you and repeat it over and over as you lull yourself to sleep; such as repeating the words "success and wealth." With this thought for example, there is little chance of conflict in your mind as there would be by saying, "I want a million dollars now." To be a little clearer perhaps, there is little chance of developing any sub-vocal arguing caused by the phrase "success and wealth." Whereas, there may be an internal argument by saying something like, "I want a million dollars." In other words, continue to be aware during and after affirming a thought. Did you follow it up with a negating thought or subtle negating argument? When you have a negating thought, cancel it. Say to yourself, "This is just a nuisance fantasy of my own imagination. I created it, and therefore, I can send it away." Or, as my son would say, "Clear that." Do not let this trouble you. I have found that in time it does not matter, because the repetition of your heart's desire will win out, if you just persist in asking, with faith and taking action.

Consciously creating and affirming words of prosperity, health, wealth, love, peace, and perfect self-expression, must bring them about into your life. Say your words of good with a strong desire, and feel that you have received your requested desire.

You may choose to speak your desires/affirmations aloud or to yourself. You may choose to do so as though you are actually talking to someone else. For example, you might use God, your Higher-Self, Infinite Intelligence, the Universe, or a made-up trusted friend within your own mind.

Some of the following affirmations, of which I use, are a derivative of versions from the writings of other authors.

Reduce your goal/desire to one, two, or three clearly stated sentences and repeat it daily. Hold the thought often throughout the day, (from the section "Goal Setting…) or at least when you awaken and before you go to be sleep.

You may want to begin with one goal/desire at a time, or as Robert Sheinfeld suggests, "Ask for everything."

Affirmations

*   I would like to have many friends and acquaintances with whom to enjoy my life; who are fun and who are interesting to me. I desire to have friends who care about themselves; friends who care about my well-being.
*   As I change all conditions change. Everyday in everyway, my life is better and better.
*   I desire to have closer family relationships.
*   Infinite Spirit, relieve me of all my fears and doubts. Only that which is true about God my Father, is true about me. My Father and I are one.
*   I desire success and abundance in my life and I am ready to accept it now.
*   Whatsoever I shall ask, I shall receive with ease, in perfect ways, under Grace.
*   I vow to seek to be carefree, enthusiastic, compassionate, and loving.
*   "Infinite Spirit, open the way for the Divine Design of my life to manifest: Let the genius within me now be released; let me see clearly the perfect plan" (Shinn). I am always under direct inspiration; I make right decision quickly.
*   Bless this car and everyone I interact with on these streets.
(This also helps me to remember to have patience with others while I drive)

* Thank you for helping me to become an excellent…
* I desire to earn $ xxxxx, or more, for the work I love to do…
* Thank you for guiding me in the way in which you know is best for me to receive…that which I desire.
* I am of great service to my fellow man…
* My Father recreates me, cell-by-cell, minute-by-minute, and brings me closer and closer to perfect health in body and mind.
* Every man is a golden link in the chain of my success.
* I strongly desire to bring my conscious mind and my subconscious mind together in harmony. (My ego, id, and super-ego)

An ending for any affirmation: I wish these desires fulfilled with ease, in perfect ways, under Grace.

One of my daily Affirmations

Thank you for helping me daily to overcome all of my fears and doubts.

Thank you for guiding me to people and opportunities that leads me to find peace, love, abundance, and prosperity.

Infinite spirit, open the way for the Devine Design of my life to manifest. Miracle shall follow miracle and wonders shall never cease. That I see clearly the perfect plan for my life.

What God has done for others He now does for me and more.

Devine Love floods my consciousness and every cell in my body.

Happiness

It was many years ago when I took my first college philosophy class. At that time the introductory course was called, Philosophy 101. Philosophy is the search for truth. This is the kind of a class that makes you look at the people from the past who asked the tough questions like: "Who am I?" "What am I doing here?" "What's it all about?" They sought metaphysical questions like: "How big is the universe?" "How did life begin?" "Is there a God?" "Is there life after death?" "Do I have a soul?" "Where did soul come from and where does it go?"

I remember that one of the first questions the professor asked the class was, "What is man's number one goal?" No one answered so then he asked, "Well, what is it that you want the most in life?" That time he did get some answers from the students, like love, peace, health, wealth, et cetera.

Then, he went on to say something that sounded like it had a lot of merit. He said, "Man's number one goal in life is to attain happiness." Disturbingly, he went on to say that everything we do, we do to bring ourselves to that end. But the problem, as he put it is that happiness is ephemeral. We find happiness, then we lose the feeling of happiness, and then we do something to find it again. Being the professor, every time someone would challenge him he would support his argument very well.

He went on to reiterate the statement that "Everything we do, we do to make ourselves happy." Now every time someone would dispute this statement with a scenario, again he would present a good argument to support his claim. Example: "If I buy my wife a dress, it is to make her happy," would be a challenge that a student would present. To paraphrase as I remember it, the professor would respond with something such as: If your wife didn't like the dress that you spent your hard earned money on and much of your time looking for it, wouldn't you feel disappointed and maybe hurt? On the other hand, wouldn't it make you happy if she simply loved it? Then, didn't you actually go through all of that effort for yourself? That is to say that you bought the dress for your wife hoping that she would appreciate you, and isn't that to make yourself happy?

He went on with many analogies such as taking care of your children, buying presents for loved ones at Christmas and birthdays, gifts for that special intimate friend, so on, and et cetera. He never let up; "You do these things because it makes you feel good. It brings you happiness when you do something that others in your life benefit from, and that is the reason you do these things."

For many years to follow, and because of that professor, I believed there was nothing that neither I nor any human did that was not motivated by the drive to achieve happiness for one's self. This seemed healthy enough though. People I cared about benefiting from me trying to make myself happy.

The negative side of this of course, is living to try to make other people happy so that I could be temporarily happy. So I took the attitude that I would do the things that I liked to do. I found that being selfish was a good thing. I would then continue to consider being self-centered as a negative attitude. My attitude became that if I did things for others because I wanted to, then they would benefit from my kindness. This gave me a good feeling; therefore, I would feel happy. If I did things for myself, I would be happy and the people around me would benefit. Again, because I was happy, I was pleasant to be around me.

Over the years I found that this behavior did not really address the issue of happiness, that is to say, why happiness was so temporary.

It took me many years to overcome the notion of, "We only do things to make ourselves happy," with something that for me made so much more sense. **I believe happiness is a state of being.** It is our birthright to be happy. We can be happy for no reason!

A few years ago I found that being happy does not necessitate relying on external causes. In fact, relying on an external cause to be happy is why happiness is so elusive and short lived. For example, if someone special to you gives you something like their love, this could be a good reason to be happy. If that someone special to you takes that love away, is that not cause to be unhappy? Again, if you find something that makes you happy, then losing it, rightfully, can make you feel unhappy as well. Anything that is given to you that makes you happy can be taken away or lost, leaving you to feel unhappy. Therefore, if you have no reason to be happy and accept the fact that you can be happy without a reason, then you can live in that state of happiness naturally.

This is not just semantics. Give this concept some contemplation. Happiness is a state of being; it is your birthright, and not dependent on external factors. It is part of who you are and what you are. It is not a feeling, yet there is evenness and calm to your persona that you can sense even outside of the practice of meditation. It is like having a small constant smile inside of you. It just is!

Follow this thought carefully. Feelings of joy and sadness are real expressions of your being. They are conditional on how you respond to external events. Like anyone, I have these feelings too. Joy is a positive feeling I receive or the result of a harmonious exchange in a relationship with someone or something in my environment. And to make this short, sadness comes with negative causes. Recognition of these feelings, and recognition of this state of "being happy" is what this means. The recognition and understanding of this state of being, also helps to keep the reactions one may have to these feelings from being overwhelming and over reactive.

Yes in reality, you can be happy for no reason. Look inside yourself and begin to recognize who you are.

"Leaders are Readers"

If you are going to lead others or you are intent on "leading your own life," read what other people have to say on any subject that is your field of interested.

Leaders read about the things other people have to say (for many reasons). The most important reasons to me are: So I can find correct knowledge that will support or encourage what I believe, and that which I teach. From reading what others have written, I might find something new to add to the evolutionary growth of my life. I might change to see and understand another view or opposing view.

As I have stated in other words, some of mankind's greatest leaders are formally educated. Some of them are not. Those who are not formally educated know the value of learning. They do study everything they need to know to become and stay successful in their fields. They both do have one thing very much in common, and that is, desire!

I make this next comment as having been a reading teacher, so I might have a bias, but I say it with all sincerity. I strongly urge you to read as a part of your personal growth effort, even if only to sharpen or refresh your reading skills. Reading is one of the most important skills to learn and practice. It affords each of us communication of ideas from people with whom we may never otherwise meet in this life. There are books written on everything you can imagine. If you practice reading you can learn about anything of your heart's desire.

Suggested Readying

My sincere thanks to all of these Writers and Teachers

The works from various religious scriptures are interwoven and quoted throughout most of the following writings.

Robert Sheinfeld, *Invisible Path to Success*

John-Roger, *Spiritual Warrior*

Stephen Covey, *The 7 Habits of Highly Successful People*

Florence Scovel-Shinn, *Wisdom of Florence Scovel-Shinn (Anthology)*

Napoleon Hill, *Keys to Success; Think and Grow Rich;*
        You Can Work Your Own Miracle.

Joseph Murphy, *The Power of the Subconscious Mind; The Miracle of Mind Dynamics*

Deepak Chopra, *Seven Spiritual Laws of Success*

Karen Alexander, *A Gift from Daniel*

John Randolph Price, *Empowerment; Self Mastery*

Carlos Warter, *Who do You Think You Are?*

Emmet Fox, *The Sermon On The Mount: The Key to Success In Life*

William M. Berliner, *Managerial and Supervisory Practice: cases and principles.*

Og Mandino, *The Greatest Salesman*

Wayne Dyer, *Your Sacred Self; You'll See It When You Believe It*

U.S. Anderson, *Three Magic Words*

The following materials are more esoteric.

Paramahansa Yogananda, *Autobiography of a Yogi*

Thick Naht Hahn, *Miracle of Mindfulness*

D.T. Suzuki, *An Introduction to Zen Buddhism*

Anthony J. Fisichella, *Echoes From Eternity*

Neale Donald Walsch, *Conversations With God; Book 1*

Carlos Castaneda, *The Teachings of Don Juan*

Bobbie Tyler, *The Key*

Kahlil Gibran, *The Prophet*

Ruby Nelson, *The Door of Everything*

Edward LeJoly and Jaya Chaliha, *Reaching out in Love: Stories told by Mother Teresa*

SECTION FIVE

Autobiography

"I am a man like any other." (Quai Chain Kane)

Because it was my desire that the reader get right into the meat of the material at hand, I decided to put my story at the end of this book. For those who may be interested in reading about the writer, well here I am. I feel that this book is not about me. It is about what we can do with our lives. Again, my intention is to carry on the legacy of wisdom that our ancestors, our predecessors wanted to us to have. In order that along the way while building and creating a wonderful life for ourselves, we start to look at just who we really are. My hope is that this, that our legacy will inspire you to seek out who you really are, and to develop your personal power for your highest good as well.

I am reluctant to write my life story, not because my life is not important enough; it is to me, but because, I want to focus your attention on what you too can do with your life. Understand that no matter what you have done in the past, or what your position in life is now, it is yours to do with as you please.

I was told, but I do not remember by whom, people like to know something about the author to see if they can relate to him or her. I was told that by one's reading a bio, the reader might get an idea of where the author is "coming from." Therefore, I will gladly share with you a sketch of my life.

My life, this time, started in Italy where I was born. My parents immigrated to America when I was eleven months old. Basically, for my parents, it was the old story of moving to the "Land of Opportunity." They left everything they knew behind to start anew in this country. That is what you did back then, to do the best you could for your family.

For as long as I can remember we were poor, but I never really felt poor. About the time I was five years old, my father managed to buy a home for us in Chicago. We always seemed to have enough to eat. I guess it was because of their simple diet and the way my mother cooked that there always seemed to be plenty of food.

Clothes, hand-me-downs mostly, were always clean and stitched if they needed to be. But I did not know any better for a long time.

School was not my forte. But then, I was always told that by my teachers and by my parents. "Oh he's smart, but he's lazy." "He daydreams and doesn't pay attention." I heard this most of my growing years. It was no wonder that I did not go to college back in those days. Nevertheless, I knew had to do something when I graduated high school.

The predominant concept of the time was; you had to get through high school or you would have no future. College was only for those who were to attain greater heights. You also, had to get a job and raise a family and that was it. That was life then and that is the way it was.

Well, I was not very rebellious, and I could not think of a job that I might like to spend my life rotting away at, so I joined the Air Force. At first glance that was not the safest career move to make; the Viet Nam war was…well that is another story. It was a terrible point in history for America, as well as for Viet Nam. But I did not worry; it was what you did back then, mindlessly follow like sheep. Looking back, I can easily see how Grace covered me and kept me safe, while hundreds of thousands of men and women died.

I went through basic training in Texas, then I was shipped off to technical school back in Illinois, and then to Kansas for permanent duty. I never got out of Kansas until I was discharged from the service and returned home to Chicago.

The last year in service I did the other part of the ideal for that era. I got married and started a family. You know, "that's" what was expected.

Let me extend my thanks to the Air Force for teaching me a trade that I could carry into civilian life. I learned to be an aircraft mechanic and went back home to Chicago with my family after my military discharge.

Within a couple of years of bouncing around and trying to make ends meet, raising a family, and proving I would not amount to anything, I finally got a job as a janitor with a major airline. That was, as it were, all I needed to get my life moving forward.

I did not like being a janitor, but that was the start offered to me at the time. I did enjoy many of its aspects and I did the best I could do with the job. At least I was in the airline industry, and I had hoped to work on airplanes as a mechanic again someday.

After some time had past, and with a leave of absence from my job, I took a ten-day test refresher course that took me thirty days to complete. Nevertheless, I did complete it and with that, I obtained my federal license to work on commercial aircraft. Within two years thereafter, my family and I moved to Florida where I would accept a promotion to aircraft mechanic with the same company I had been working with in Chicago.

I finally got a career start and I was on the move to yuppie-dom. By this time I had been married for five years. Those years, if you will imagine, had many difficult moments.

Let us move forward in time a little. Sometime after settling into my new surroundings at my job in Florida, I met a man at work who started me on my journey to real-life magic. What he introduced me to was the magic of making a better and more peaceful life for myself. His name was Dave. That puts us at about 1977.

I had always been interested in mystical things, magic and fantasy. In the back of my mind I felt like there had to be some real-life magical power somewhere. It could not be just a romantic notion past down in ancient myths. Just look at the control the martial artist exhibit, the yogis, and all of those wonderful stories of people with amazing abilities from ancient times to the present.

Dave was the first person to acquaint me with Kriya Yoga and Paramahansa Yogananda's book, *Autobiography of a Yogi*.

Dave was quite a role-model for me; a peaceful man. He handled some very stressful situations well, all due to his faith and convictions. This book he introduced me to, in itself, started me on my path. By the way, at this point in my life, early on in my studies and practice of yoga meditation, I wondered how anyone who could find this much peace in life would ever stop the practice of living this philosophy. Dave suggested to me that people are people and we can easily get distracted. Dave died some ten years after we had met, and I continue to be very grateful that he came into my life.

My advice to you is, if you choose this path do not wonder; stay amazed. Do not wander either. I stepped off this path. I stepped away from living in peace and harmony.

I now, in reflection, distinctly remember going about my business in my new lifestyle, vegetarian and all, about two years later or so, I got involved in a business venture. I had not seen much of Dave at all during this time. We had moved into separate departments at work. Somewhere around that time I made the comment to myself pertaining to this path, "I'll do this later; I've got a full-time job and a business to run." That was the time that marked going back to my rush to succeed. That was not a good turning point in my life.

In the following four years I was in divorce and bills up to my neck, as I struggled to keep my head above water, while trying to keep my sanity.

All along the road there are people who are willing to help you through your struggle. Sometimes you just need to look up. Then, there are those people who do not mean to enjoy your misery, but they do. They will help you to help it last. It becomes a sort of a soap opera for them to "loom over."

Just when I thought I was making headway with my life and my bills, about five years later, I then lost my job. I had already relinquished over to my ex-wife, the business we had built together. And now, I had some major overhauling of my life to do, again. But first, I had to go through, "The Old Identity Crisis." By this time I had seventeen years of identifying myself to my job (Now what would Yogananda have recommended doing?).

I knew I was not going to be able to get through this episode in my life by myself, so I sought help. I found a wonderful counselor through the V.A. My counselor, Bobby, and to whom I am also still grateful, encouraged and directed me to pull my life back together. He helped me to remember the feelings of peace I once had back in the days when I was more grounded in meditation. That was when I began to get back on track to my path, little-by-little; struggle mixed with peace.

But it had taken nearly fourteen years more for me to make a sincere effort to find out how to become really successful in life. I do not count my successes in real estate sales nearly as important anymore. What success means to me is, "Creating my life to be as I desire it to be." That is real magic, and that is real power. This power is based on these simple statements passed down to us by our predecessors; "Ask and you shall receive." And, "What you think about, you bring about." You must study what these simple statements mean and how they work. Why they work is because it is your birthright to have such an awesome power. You were born with the ability to create your life to be as you desire it to be.

Study and then practice that which you study. Just like anything else you would want to become good at doing, be it management, engineering, architecture, repair, sales, or teaching, what ever you desire to do with your life. You have to study and then practice what you have studied.

Here is a clue: Life flows more freely when you are working at what you love doing and asking your other-self for help and guidance. If you are finding a great deal of resistance in achieving peace in what you are doing, perhaps you will need to reassess your goals and intentions.

As I had mentioned real estate, let me tell you how it related to the material in this book.

I began my real estate career unwittingly and under capitalized. I could not put a deal together for the entire first six months that I was in the business. I can easily recall, in reflection, much of my sub-vocalization during that time. It all boiled down to this, "I wasn't good enough to become a success."

I learned to do my job well, but I can see now both my fear of failure and fear of success. For example, on my way to meet with a potential client, I would come up with all sorts of negating thoughts about the outcome of the meeting, literally including, "Gee, I hope they don't show up," and most often they would not. In those days of course, I would blame them for wasting my time, for not keeping our appointment. My subconscious was not against me, (I) it would always arrange for my desires with all the resources it has in the universe with which to work.

While working in real estate, too often I would really say things like, "I love this work so much, I'd do it for free." And often, I would advise people on what they needed to do for the sale or purchase of a home and then let them do it with some other realtor.

Still not fully understanding the mechanism involved, and after six months of struggle, I began **acting** like some of the more successful people I had met in my chosen field and things started happening for me. Of course, my sub-vocalization was changing as well.

As I was becoming more and more successful in real estate, and because I was becoming more involved in my community, I started to grow more introspectively. Realizing that at times I felt as though I was being guided along, although I did not understand what was going on with me back then as well as I do now. Truly this only meant I was reflecting more and becoming more aware.

In my last year of work in real estate sales I went back to college to study in business administration. I continued to do volunteer service in the public school system. Along the way I beat the national average for deals per month in real estate, but all the time I was being drawn into teaching, or guided.

Well to make a very long story much shorter, I graduated from college with a degree in business. In time, I went on to the university and received my degree in teaching. Shortly thereafter, I left real estate sales to become a teacher. At first I had my regrets about my decision to leave real estate and go into teaching, but not anymore. I studied and practiced what I have discussed in this book, and began to recreate my life.

As my life started to change, "coincidentally," I had said that when I could prove to myself that asking with purpose on purpose is truth, I would write a book that might encourage others to do the same.

As for a few examples I said to the Universe; I desired to develop a life that would bring me health, wealth, love, and perfect self-expression, under grace. I asked that everything I ask for I shall receive with ease, in perfect ways, under Grace. I said that I desired to teach at a college and at an adult community school. I asked that a wonderful, loving woman, with desires and goals that are in alignment with my own, to come into my life. All of these desires have been fulfilled.

At the time that I originally wrote this book I taught adults in the public school system and as an adjunct professor at a private college. And yes, relationships are also built on the law of attraction and how we ask. I believe there are many wonderful lessons and experiences to be gained when you open yourself up to being involved in sincere relationships. All of this and more has come to me, in accordance with my change of thinking and the consistent use of affirmations on purpose with purpose.

Let me leave you with this. Your life and your surroundings are literally a reflection of how you think. Life is meant to be free flowing and wonderful. This is your birthright. Herein lies what I have learn about this ancient wisdom. Practice asking your Subconscious, Higher Self, Universal Intelligence, or God for everything. State your desires. Do what you love doing and you will always have enough. You will always have enough money, friends, travel, and whatever is your heart's desire. Of this I am certain. Become certain for yourself.

God blessed all of us with a tremendous Gift. What will you do with your Gift?

Summary of Facts

Fact: You can be happy for no reason. Therefore, no one can take this state of being away from you.

Fact: What you identify with is what you are. What you start to identify with is what you become. Identify with Health, Wealth, Love, and Perfect Self-expression.

Fact: Ask, believing and you shall receive.

Fact: The power is yours to use. Thought, desire, purpose, intention, emotion, faith, and action, are all you need to achieve what you **will**.

Fact: Negating thoughts cancel out your positive desires. Everyone with whom I have met that lives in peace and is successful, has reduced much of their negative thinking. Create a desire and then get out of your own way. Have faith, and trust that your desires will be fulfilled.

Fact: Negative thoughts attract negative experiences. Your subconscious mind does not second-guess you. It is literally the same as asking your subconscious mind to bring you negative experiences. They are after all, your thoughts.

Fact: Your habit thinking brings about your daily experiences as they are. If you do not like the way your life is going, look to the way you think about the things you think about, as often as possible. Therein lies a strong indication of how you see things to be. This is like, the attitude you have about people and things. How do you see the world around you? What do you think about the people around you?

Fact: You have total control over your own mind. You can think as you will and change the way you think, if you will.

Fact: Your subconscious mind has tremendous resources to help you to accomplish any desire you may have. You just have to ask, believing and act with faith that it will be done.

Fact: Your subconscious mind is always listening to you and bringing you your life as it IS through your habit thinking. From the seemingly insignificant to the most amazing things you can imagine to have come into your life. Practice asking for everything; with ease, in perfect ways, under Grace. Prove it for yourself!

Fact: Your thoughts create your environment as you believe the world to be, and not vice versa.

Fact: Energy follows thought to create what ever you desire. You and your surroundings are literally a reflection of your habit thinking. How are you thinking? How does the world appear to you personally? If you do not like what you see or the way things are going for you right now, then make changes in your thinking toward what you would rather have in your life.

Fact: God, your Higher Self, Divine Intelligence, the Universe or whatever you wish to call It, wants you to achieve your heart's desires. It does not care what you call It, because It is everything. It is The All That Is.

Fact: You do not have to be relieved of all your negative thinking to be able to create a more peaceful and more successful life. Keep affirming your desires. Practice with faith and patience. It is your birthright to consciously create your life to be as you desire it to be. Plant the seed (your desire), nurture it and watch it grow over time. "What you think about, you bring about."

Fact: From a certain point of view, negative and positive thoughts and experiences are neither negative nor positive. They are just your thoughts and experiences. For everyday living, in our reality, suffice it to say that a negative is something that you do not like or condone, and a positive is something you do like or want to have in your life.

This book is a study of but one aspect of life. It is, in my view, only one of the many aspects of creation that makes life so wonderfully challenging and so interesting.

I have written about what I have learned, which has helped me to recreate my life to be something immensely more satisfying.

I have written this book to pass along the legacy of ancient wisdom. My hope is to encourage others to seek knowledge, truth, and the power. It is our Divine Right to have and to use this power. The proof is in doing. Prove it to yourself!

As you move forward along your path of life seeking truth, you will begin to get a sense of who you really are, and perhaps you will lay claim to your Divine Right.

Bless you!

Meditation

In this edition I have included a meditation technique that I use and enjoy.

If you are not familiar with meditation techniques, let me advise that you read all of the way through the following information at least once prior to applying yourself to this exercise.

A friend introduced me to Kriya Yoga many years ago. Kriya Yoga devotees are intensely disciplined and the study is very involved. You can find Kriya Yoga on the World Wide Web if you are interested in learning more about it.

In this case, I am offering a meditation practice that may help you to achieve quiet and stillness with many benefits. Though comparatively rudimentary, this exercise is very effective in re-energizing the body, relieving stress, encouraging a peaceful attitude, and developing better concentration skills.

The practice of sitting quietly and emptying your mind can become frustrating, because the mind is always seeking to be busy. During this exercise it would be uncommon, at first, for unwanted random thoughts to enter your mind. Mostly because the initial preparation for this meditation is more then enough to keep your mind occupied.

First: Choose an area to meditate that is not distracting. Some areas of your home, such as the bedroom for example, are easily related to other daily habit activities and may make meditating difficult. In most cases, the bedroom is where we spend a great deal of time and so we do not relate it to a place to meditate. Although, dedicating a corner of your bedroom for the sole purpose of your place to meditate, may work very well for you. As you become adept at meditating, you will find that you can meditate pretty much anywhere. But in the beginning at least, avoid meditating on your bed or lying down on your back. This makes it too easy to fall asleep as you practice meditating. In meditation you want to be aware of being. Sleep does not often lend itself to this experience.

Other choices of where to meditate may be your garden, porch, patio, attic or basement. You may find it comfortable to meditate in a church, temple, synagogue or a quiet park where you know you will not be disturbed.

Second: Sit yourself in a comfortable position of your choice. For those who are familiar with Yoga, you may be comfortable in the Lotus or Zen postures. These are excellent resting positions that help to keep the spinal column comfortably erect. Or, you may be comfortable just sitting on the ground with your legs crossed. Yes, you may sit on a chair or on a bench as well. In any of these positions you must work on relaxing the physical aspects of the body first and "being still."

Begin the second portion of the exercise by holding your back in an erect position, but not rigid, with your chin parallel to the ground. If you are sitting on a chair avoid leaning back. Sit erect, and from this point on, practice not moving; practice "being still."

In your mind tell your body to relax and then notice the change.

For example, make a tight fist. Feel the tension. Relax your fist; now relax it more, and yet more. Feel the tension melt away and then release it even more. If at first you do not recognize a difference between the tension and the release, try it again.

You may tell portions of your body to relax. You might begin by telling your shoulders to relax, and then notice the change from tense to loose, or at least less tense. Continue by telling each of the major muscle groups in your body, in turn, to relax and then notice the change.

From this relaxation and stillness practice of the meditation exercise, you may notice sensations like your body may become tingly, light, very heavy and sinking, or as though your body is not there. These are all common effects of this portion of the exercise.

It may take you some time to become accustom this practice. All in all, a feeling of physical calm should prevail over your entire being. This calm will also extend itself to your mental well-being. You might work on bringing yourself to this point of calm a few times before you venture further. In other words, after you have found the right place and the right position for you to meditate, you might choose to practice only this aspect for a while in the beginning.

Third: Now that you have attained a feeling of calm and stillness, you may start to concentrate on your breathing. Breathing is a very important facet of meditation. It is said that the secret to achieving success in meditation comes from controlling the breath. There are four aspects, or phases, to one cycle of breathing. They are inhalation, holding the inhalation, exhalation, and holding the exhalation.

When breathing in, air is taken in through the nose filling the lungs from the bottom up, like you would fill a bottle with water. This is breathing to the diaphragm; to the bottom of the lungs so to speak.

Note: To help you to become aware, and to help you to direct your breath to your diaphragm, you may try lying on your back. Though I cautioned earlier, avoid meditating lying on your back, strictly for its physical aspect, this may help you to practice controlling your breath.

From this position place one hand on your stomach region and the other on your chest. As you begin the breathing exercise, you would be able to notice that only the hand on your stomach is moving up and down as you inhale and exhale. When you feel that you are comfortably controlling the flow of your breathing, return to the meditation posture you have chosen previously. Relax your body once again and then begin the breathing portion of the exercise once again.

Note: Before you begin the cycle of breathing, take in a deep breath through your nose and exhale through your mouth. Do not rush and repeat it one more time. Expand your lungs and exhale, but do not rush, yawn if you feel the need to yawn and fill your lungs.

The cycle of inhalation, holding the inhalation, exhalation, and holding the exhalation is done very slowly; approximately 5 to 10 seconds for each phase. Remember to breathe to the diaphragm expanding the region of the stomach and then collapsing that region on exhalation. Slowly remove all of the air from your lungs that you can, but do not force it. Repeat this cycle as many times as you can comfortably, until you are able to repeat this cycle 10 times. You may notice that it will take longer to exhale slowly and empty your lungs than it did to slowly fill them.

When this portion of the exercise is complete, begin to breathe at a normal rate and continue to breathe to the diaphragm. This is done in a fashion that may remind you of a pendulum. Again, breathe at a normal rate; inhale, hesitate, exhale, hesitate, and just breathe in a relaxed manner.

Just getting accustom to this exercise may take a little more time at first. As you learn to relax and take control over your body, you will be able to take your meditation position with ease and in much less time. The breathing exercise will become less laborious with practice.

Forth: Initially you may find that since you have put so much attention on taking control of your relaxation and breathing, you were not bothered by random thoughts. But now that the physical portion of your meditation exercise has become easier, the thoughts will again come and again try to gain your attention. For example, those of you who when you first started to drive a car, your mind was intensely occupied with driving. Now most of the times when you get into your car you hardly think of the driving aspect. We call this "second nature" and your mind thinks of many things aside from driving your car. As you practice meditation do not become disturbed by these thoughts that beckon your attention, just gently bring yourself back to your meditation. To avoid paying attention to the random thoughts that are trying to gain the attention of your mind, focus! You may put your attention once again on relaxation, on your breathing or on your heartbeat. You may take control of your mind by putting your attention on your blood pulsing throughout your body to the rhythm of your heartbeat. This is yet another way to regain control of your mind to reduce the random thoughts that may distract you. When you arise from this meditation, take your time getting up. Do not get up quickly. You will start to feel refreshed, rested and energized.

Finally: As you become adept and comfortable at meditating in this fashion, the random thoughts will again continue to flow. Do not give in to these thoughts. By that I mean, do not latch on to any one thought and give it your attention.

There is a calm, quiet, empty space in your consciousness. Rest your mind there, in that empty space. It is the space between your thoughts. This is meditation. This space is like the end to a sentence, and then there is a pause, and then the next sentence. The pause is the empty space, like the space between your thoughts. Your thoughts are like a series of seemingly never ending sentences. But all thoughts, like sentences, have an end, a period, a pause.

Gently place your conscious mind on that quiet place between your thoughts and feel the peace and tranquility. Hold this place as long as you can. You can become the observer. You may bask in the calm and enjoy the peace. It may be for only split seconds at first. When you find yourself thinking of something, do not let yourself become annoyed, take control and just gently place your consciousness back into that space between your thoughts.

There are several relaxation and meditation methods. Find one that is comfortable for you and make it one of your healthy daily habits.

Remember, **"Be still and know that I am God"** (**Psalm 46:10**)

Author's note

Since the first edition of <u>Legacy: The Power Within</u> was released in February of 2001, I have continued to study and change my life for the better.

Yes, here in 2004, I still practice exercising the power within me; asking for and receiving many wonderful things and experiences in my life.

Make time to become aware of who you really are; of your spirit and your relationship to All That Is. See where this journey may lead you.

Hold your best wishes close to your heart and watch what happens.

Legacy: The Power Within
www.powerlegacy.com

0-595-13520-X